A WOMAN OF INFLUENCE

'Everything is biographical. There is a hidden presence of others in us, even those we have known briefly. We contain them for the rest of our lives.'

Michael Ondaatje, *Divisadero*, 2007

A WOMAN OF INFLUENCE

SCIENCE, MEN & HISTORY

ANN MOYAL

UWA PUBLISHING

First published in 2014 by
UWA Publishing
Crawley, Western Australia 6009
www.uwap.uwa.edu.au

UWAP is an imprint of UWA Publishing
a division of The University of Western Australia

THE UNIVERSITY OF
WESTERN AUSTRALIA

This book is copyright. Apart from any fair dealing for the purpose of private study, research, criticism or review, as permitted under the *Copyright Act 1968*, no part may be reproduced by any process without written permission. Enquiries should be made to the publisher.

National Library of Australia
Cataloguing-in-Publication entry

Author: Moyal, Ann, 1926- author.

Title: A woman of influence : science, men & history / Ann Moyal.

ISBN: 9781742585970 (paperback)

Subjects: Moyal, Ann, 1926-
Scholar—Australia—Biography.
Women scholars—Australia--Biography.
Historians—Australia—Biography.
Women historians—Australia—Biography.

Dewey Number: 994.007202

Cover image: *Ann Moyal*, 1957, Pamela Thalben Ball (1927-2012), oil on canvas. Collection: National Portrait Gallery, Canberra. Gift of Ann Moyal 2012. Donated through the Australian Government's Cultural Gifts Program.

Printed by Lightning Source

BOOKS BY THE AUTHOR

A Guide to the Records of Australian Science. (Australian Academy of Science and ANU Press, 1966)

Scientists in Nineteenth Century Australia: A Documentary History. (Cassell Australia, Sydney, 1976)

Clear Across Australia: A history of telecommunications. (Thomas Nelson, Australia, Melbourne, 1984)

'A Bright & Savage Land': Scientists in Colonial Australia. (Collins, Sydney, 1986; Penguin Books, 1993)

Portraits in Science. Compiled, edited and introduced by Ann Moyal. (National Library of Australia, Canberra, 1994)

Breakfast with Beaverbrook: Memoirs of an Independent Woman. (Hale & Iremonger, Sydney, 1995)

Platypus: The Extraordinary Story of How a Curious Creature Baffled the World. (Allen & Unwin, St. Leonards, 2001, 2nd edition 2010; Smithsonian Institution, Washington DC, 2001; John Hopkins University Press, Baltimore, Maryland, 2004)

The Web of Science: The Scientific Correspondence of the Rev W. B. Clarke, Australia's Pioneer Geologist. 2 volumes. (Australian Scholarly Publishing, Melbourne, 2003)

Alan Moorehead: A Rediscovery. (National Library of Australia, Canberra, 2005)

Maverick Mathematician: The life and science of J. E. Moyal. (ANU E Press, Canberra, 2006)

Koala: A Historical Biography. (CSIRO Publishing, 2008)

CONTENTS

INTRODUCTION

1. A SENSE OF PLACE

2. BEING A HISTORIAN

3. THE YELLOW RUG. THE STORY OF A MARRIAGE

4. GENESIS. THE INDEPENDENT SCHOLARS ASSOCIATION OF AUSTRALIA

5. A LATE LOVE

6. AMONG THE HISTORIANS

7. DYMPHNA. 'THE GIRL IN THE DIRNDL DRESS'

8. MEETING ALAN MOOREHEAD

9. THE WRITERS' HOUSE

10. 'A LONG CHAIN OF CLEVER PEOPLE'

11. THE AUSTRALIAN ARK

12. 'THE BOTTOM LINE'

13. WRITING 'MR CLARKE'

14. 'ONLY CONNECT'

15. OLD AGE

16. OUT OF THE WEST

17. WAVING TO BEAVERBROOK

EPILOGUE

INTRODUCTION

During 1995 I published my autobiographical *Breakfast with Beaverbrook. Memoirs of an Independent Woman*. It was at a time when, in my mid-sixties, I believed I had done it all. But later in that decade I came upon a telling commentary by American literary academic Carolyn Heilbrun (who long doubled as the engaging detective fiction-writer Amanda Cross) that held these words: 'Whenever I read the story of an autobiography of an older woman – and they are rare enough, I find that though it is written by a woman in her fifties and beyond, she writes only to go back to her youth. She abandons age, experience, wisdom to search the past, usually for romance, always for the beginnings in childhood'. 'For me', Heilbrun added, 'the stories of youth are tired stories. But the story of age, of maturity before infirmity, before meaningless old age, has never been told except perhaps by Shakespeare who told everything, provided he could tell it of men'.

I suspect as that decade moved into the next, this may no longer be the case. Two Australian works of recent years, Inga Clendinnen's *Tiger's Eye*, and Brenda Niall's *Life Class: The Education of a Biographer*, in part challenge Heilbrun's claim, although they are full-life journeys. The crop of memoirs by three Australian women with their resonantly feminist titles, Susan Ryan's *Catching the Waves*, Anne Summers' *Ducks on the Pond*, and

Wendy McCarthy's *Don't Fence Me In* – published within a year of each other at the century's turn, are essentially from the pens of women in mid-flight, vivid in their younger and working careers.

My original impetus to autobiography arose from the fact that contemporary memoirs in Australia had appeared exclusively from the pens of men, where women found place only as mistresses or wives. But as I had enjoyed an intellectual's life, there seemed good reason to add another perspective. More importantly, I'd also had a historian's life centred on a series of what I saw as 'encounters with history'. Working in the 1950s with the charismatic and powerful Lord Beaverbrook, at a time when he was closely in touch with his old friend Sir Winston Churchill and had himself turned to the writing of history, was a chronicle in itself. Yet I had written the book mainly, I thought, for a professional women's audience. My sister and I had paced along a leafy path in Sydney devising its purposeful subtitle, and in press interviews following its publication I had spoken often of the continuing prevalence in Australia of a patriarchy in professional and public affairs that had contributed to a significant devaluation of women in this country.

I was therefore delighted when the book had a wider appeal. The Australian Broadcasting Commission presented it as a television documentary in their January 1997 series of six 'Life Stories', where, in the creative hands of Brian Nicholls as director, and the familiar background voice of Justin Murphy, it told of my happy family childhood; my graduation in history from Sydney University; my years in England and abroad working and travelling with Lord Beaverbrook; my two short English marriages; and, returning as an academic to the Australian National University, my career as a historian of Australian science and my marriage to the Israeli mathematician J. E. (Joe) Moyal. It was, hence, joyfully reinforcing that my book found resonance with a diverse company of both men and women, and one man, remembering a passing meeting we had had some 40 years before, would enter my life at seventy as a companion and late love.

So having written, in maturity, of one Australian woman's spirited trajectory and her sometimes challenging encounters with history, I might have expected life to take a quieter turn. It hadn't. Rather I'd continued to spend my ageing life with passion, involvement, and intensity. So now I wished to gather together those buoyant passages and components; my chequered engagement as a historian; the richly unfolding interconnections and tapestry of people who have influenced and shaped me; love and loss; and the experience of vastly increasing age. And perchance, as Simone de Beauvoir neatly phrased it in her autobiography, *The Prime of Life*, I wished to 'put myself in question before all questions are silenced', or to grasp at the cry of Australia's irrepressible octogenarian artist, the remarkable Margaret Olley, 'Hurry Last Days!'

This, then, is a different story.

CHAPTER 1

A SENSE OF PLACE

I have been in love with Canberra for over sixty years. Its parched landscape, its ring of deep blue mountains etched against an iridescent sky, its light and calming beauty and the fiery brilliance of its autumn days colour my mind and spirit and anchor me firmly in this beautiful place.

As early as 1912, it seems, I had been latched, prenatally, into the 'bush capital'. My mother, Doss Thomas, was the niece by marriage of Canberra's founding surveyor, Charles Scrivener. The young surveyor of the New South Wales Department of Lands, having lost one wife, had met and married my grandmother's sister, Mary Beatrice Harding in 1885, a short time after the two young women arrived in Sydney from England with their surgeon father. But Beatrice had died in childbirth and her son Robert was taken over for a time by my grandmother Ethel Harding and her father, and subsequently reared by Charley's third wife. Annie Scrivener, happily, bore her husband several children and their daughter Ethel became my mother's intimate friend.

Selected for his outstanding field work, Scrivener was appointed Director of Commonwealth Lands and Surveys and in 1910 given charge of choosing, mapping and defining the contours of the Australian National Territory. He chose the vast Canberra–Yass survey site and there, tall ranging Charley, with his drooping moustache and practical zeal, gathered his team of young surveyors to play a leading role on the national stage. And in that adventurous time, the two young women, Ethel and Doss, enjoyed the exciting opportunity of staying with Charley and Annie Scrivener as they took up residence in 1912 in Acton House. There my mother experienced the camaraderie of the young surveyors coming and going, and Scrivener working far into the night, while the bare stretching landscape etched an enduring mark upon her life. My attachment to Canberra was planted in pioneering soil.

Twelve years later my mother, employed as one of the first women by the Commonwealth Bank in Sydney, would marry my father, John Hurley, a fellow member of the staff and, I, a second child, appeared. Canberra, however, continued to spread its tendrils into my life. In 1942, after Japanese planes rained down death on Pearl Harbor and began the bombing of Australia at Darwin, I, well alert to my mother's passion, was despatched from Sydney to spend my final year of schooling in Canberra with the family of Scrivener's first appointed surveyor, Percy Sheaffe. And there – an unlikely wartime evacuee, as a student from Sydney's private girls' school Wenona – I exchanged my neat navy-blue uniform for one of sober grey and attended Canberra's dashingly unusual coeducational High School. I won one of Canberra's four annual scholarships to the University of Sydney that year and my course was set.

The piny scent of Canberra's hedges and the potent fragrance of eucalyptus would follow me as I travelled overseas after graduation, making me deeply nostalgic, notably at Lord Beaverbrook's villa in the south of France. When, late in 1958, I returned to Australia to the Australian National University in Canberra, after a decade's absence abroad, I was restored to my own soil. Even though I still came and went, I put my roots down in the bush capital, buying a finely designed townhouse where my study looked out upon the eucalyptus trees and the flash of bright rosellas. Life entwined with nature.

During the mid-nineties when I took up my story, my days pulsed with action. *Breakfast with Beaverbrook* was republished in paperback in 1996 and I was soon swept along on that current of media interviews — the penalty of even modest success as an author — and invitations to talk. Yet my real reputation hinged on the fact that I had established myself as a historian of Australian science. And, in that engrossing year of 1996, the National Library of Australia, then the managing overlord of an emergent Portrait Gallery of Australia at Old Parliament House, invited me to curate an exhibition of portraiture that would celebrate the achievements of Australian scientists. Seizing on Bob Hawke's imaginative exhortation, it was called 'The Clever Country. Scientists in Australia'.

What a chance! I was well versed in the marriage of art and science in the nineteenth century. I now had the opportunity of exploring the painterly heritage of scientific participants in Australia, drawing upon the collections of the National Library and art galleries, libraries, museums, universities, herbariums, scientific societies and institutions around the country.

At once there were interesting challenges. For despite the role of science and innovation as key driving forces in our society, scientists themselves had an image problem. Stop anyone in the street and ask them to name a famous sportsman, and names burst out. Invite a bystander to name an Australian scientist, and you are likely to draw a blank. And so it seemed in portraiture.

For, as an earlier Portrait Gallery exhibition, *All in the Family*, had revealed, the most likely subjects in the early decades of Australia's settlement were the governors, soldiers, judges, administrators, politicians, wealthy merchants, and the prosperous emancipists eager to claim a position for themselves in society. Like their colleagues in Britain, colonial scientists lacked the wealth, social position or motivation to enter the portraiture stakes. And so my mission became an absorbing detective hunt – one in which I would be meeting in portraiture for the first time many of the men I had long known through their discoveries and writings.

So I began my probe. My investigation took me to the major libraries and galleries and, via highly illuminating telephone conversations, to art curators tucked away in universities, museums, galleries and scientific institutions around the country. The returns were astonishing. Not only did the galleries and museums readily yield up their prizes, the search also informed curators, particularly in the universities, who, while holding lists of paintings in their care, were often uncertain who the scientists were. With the addition of some important works, my scientific army grew. The Tasmanian Museum and Gallery offered an evocative portrait of a short, top-hatted, sartorially elegant John Gould – complete with birds and gun – painted in 1840 during his tour of the eastern colonies collecting for his *Birds of Australia* and *Mammals of Australia*. The National Library of Australia offered a thoughtful portrait of the young botanist Robert Brown who – as one of the first trained naturalists to travel to Australia on Matthew Flinders' *Investigator* voyage of circumnavigation in 1801–04 – was destined for fame as the most prestigious British botanist of his age. The National Library also held portraits of the father of New South

Wales' scientific dynasty, entomologist Alexander McLeay, and the man who planted the physical and astronomical sciences in Australia, Governor Sir Thomas Brisbane. And depicted long in years at seventy-eight, wearing his clerical robes, was the father of Australian geology the Rev. W. B. Clarke in a portrait commissioned by the Royal Society of New South Wales to flag the eminence of its founder.

It was apparent that as the twentieth century dawned other processes were at work. At that time the universities and scientific institutions, with considerable foresight, were adopting the role of artistic patrons, embarking, randomly at first and with increasing commitment, to enlist distinguished Australian portrait painters to commemorate their leading men of science. Who might come my way?

From the University of Western Australia I garnered Joshua Smith's study of the founding agricultural scientist Sir George Currie. The National Gallery of Victoria offered George Lambert's large, brilliant portrait of the eminent and influential biologist Sir Walter Baldwin Spencer. The University of Sydney brought forth its portrait of its first Professor of Anatomy, J. T. Wilson, by William Nicholson; a romantic oil portrait by James Kerr-Lawson of his brother, the first Professor of Botany; and a drawing by Louis Kahn of the mercurial Professor of Physics Harry Messel. The University of Adelaide summonsed another outstanding trio in the portraits of three famous men: Sir Douglas Mawson by Ivor Hele, Gwynne-Jones' study of Sir Howard Florey, and the life-sized figure of the powerful Sir Mark Oliphant. From Queensland University came two pictures that told a story: Gil Jamieson's lively painting of the flamboyant Professor of Veterinary Science John Francis on a prancing steed, and a portrait decked out with bottles and other scientific paraphernalia of parasitologist Professor John Sprent.

Plunging into differing provenances, my broad collection swelled. Judy Cassab's two strong portraits of the leaders of Australia's major scientific institutions – CSIRO's Sir Ian Clunies Ross and Chairman of the Australian Atomic Energy Commission, Sir Phillip Baxter – fell fruitfully into my bag. The Australian National University added June Mendoza's portrait of the physicist Vice-Chancellor Sir Leonard Huxley; a study of the much-honoured microbiologist Frank Fenner; and one of the neuroscientist Peter Bishop wearing the scientist's traditional long white coat (the only one to figure in the exhibition). The University of Melbourne brought to view Julie Edgar's sculptured head of eminent immunologist Professor Gus Nossal, and Russell Drysdale's pen-and-ink drawing of the one-armed zoologist Jack Marshall, with whom he had journeyed around Australia. I was thrilled to have brought together so rich and informing a convocation.

It came as no surprise that women subjects, notably in the nineteenth century, were very difficult to find. Science was a patriarchy and women its 'invisible participants'. What pleasure, then, to find in the National Library a glowing self-portrait of a Tasmanian botanical illustrator Sarah Fereday, painted in 1836, which represented both a wide and under-recognised sorority, and the delicate skills and artistry of this accomplished breed. The twentieth century signalled welcome winds of change. Ten portraits of twentieth-century scientific women, flushed out from universities and private collections, caught the faces and achievements of some remarkable participants. These presented CSIRO's pioneering geneticist Helen Newton Turner; a commanding portrait of Melbourne's sea-grass expert, the German wartime immigrant Sophie Ducker; the University of Tasmania's distinguished botanist Winifred Turner; the doyenne of Australian geologists, Queensland's Dorothy Hill, the first woman fellow of the Academy of Science; and two contemporary Victorian leaders, eminent biologists Professor Adrienne Clarke and Dr Nancy Millis.

Expertly hung in the spacious exhibition rooms of Old Parliament House, the collected canvases shone with life and colour and, together with their informing captions, brought a tapestry of Australia's science to view. Not only did they enhance knowledge of a diverse and talented community from our scientific past, one painting exposed a scarcely known historical fact. An oil portrait collected from a private source, painted in 1944, revealed a handsome German physicist wearing a fur-collared leather jacket, seated at his radar station on the French coast as he searched the English Channel for British planes. Dr Albert Seyler was one of several high-profile German scientists whom the Australian Government selected at the end of World War II to serve in Australia's scientific and technological institutions, in his case in telecommunications research and development at Telecom Australia where he made an outstanding contribution.

Gathering and curating, I had the great satisfaction of adding a new dimension to my historical bag. Robyn Williams sought out the exhibition, and we discussed it on his ABC 'Science Show', telling of the clever country it represented. Many centuries before, Isaac Newton declared that 'scientific discovery is built on the shoulders of giants'. Some giants were assembled here. How enlightening the work had proved. From it I cherished the simple hope that the 28,000 spectators who passed through the exhibition would perceive the men and women of Australian science less as elite, 'nerd'-like figures in laboratory coats, but as an active and talented company, seen together in a fresh and dynamic light. With its interplay of colours, its varying techniques and an unforseen range of subjects, 'The Clever Country' marked an innovative blending of science and art and afforded in itself an important backdrop to a larger sequel. Twelve years later in December 2008, Australia's new National Portrait Gallery, gleaming and elegant beside Lake Burley Griffin, opened under Andrew Sayers' direction to engage an eager and extending public and, in its wide representation of Australian life, to throw an enduring spotlight on Australian lives in science.

CHAPTER 2

BEING A HISTORIAN

As long as I can remember, which is now very long, I have been a historian. Writing history has been my beacon, my daily course, my anchor against the currents of life, my career. I write the word as a statement in my passport to affirm it in the world. Manning Clark, much given to wide deliberations, once defined the etymology of 'historian' as 'the istor', the man (no women then) 'who told the story about the past'. But the 'istor', he insisted, was no mere photographer: each must create a time, a people, and a place.

For my part, I've always had my eye on a spanning spectrum of history, although where I caught this inclination I can't be sure. For it was 'straight down the line' during my undergraduate days in history at Sydney University under the serious young lecturers John Ward and Gordon Greenwood, teaching from their prepared notes, not very far ahead of their students. We lacked the vivid approach to teaching, the questioning and challenging of methods and theory and the rich concept of the potential of history. These were the richer methods that stirred the minds of students at the Department of History at Melbourne University, where Professor Max Crawford saw it as the historian's task to look beyond the surface, to understand ideas; and in studying the sources, to become self-reflective. Crawford is described as 'an enabler who had the gift of empowering others' and he produced a notable crop of Australian historians that included the professors John Mulvaney, Hugh Stetton, Greg Dening, Ken Inglis and Graeme Davison, to name a few. At Sydney, by contrast, there was little sense that the study of history could inform both the past and the future, and shape an awareness that one could become a pioneer.

Even Stephen Roberts, among the first of that new generation of Australia's professional historians who took our honours tutorials, made little impression on my mind. Yet I proved I was good at history. I could absorb and analyse. I won the Women College's annual prize for history. But I knew nothing of the self-reflective gaze.

Having secured a two-year Research Studentship after graduating, in 1946 I was appointed Professor Roberts' research assistant when he became the University's Vice-Chancellor. It was then, through his abiding interest in the pastoral and early wine industries in Australia, that I was thrown into the green hush of the Mitchell Library. There I read the evocative, often haunting diaries of Australia's early squatters as they moved out to settle the far pastoral outposts of New South Wales, and I was hooked. It was then that I was drawn, firmly and irrevocably, into the nineteenth century's beckoning world.

But from 1949 for almost a decade in Britain my historical trajectory lured me into more contemporary affairs; first (having jettisoned my enabling scholarship at the London University's Institute of Historical Research on Pacific History) to the Institute of International Affairs at Chatham House researching Commonwealth history with the brilliant Nicholas Mansergh, and thence on to my heady days with Lord Beaverbrook, where for four glamorous years British political history and its machinations in the critical days of World War I held us in gripping thrall.

Late in 1958, however – rejecting the call to remain with the charismatic lord – I returned to my own country to work in an Australian context with another great historian Sir Keith Hancock, helping him found the *Australian Dictionary of Biography*.

There could have been no more appropriate place for my re-entry into Australian themes. For in that early work, structuring the form of a major national scholarly enterprise, a small but growing group of Australian historians were exploring the very foundations of Australia's history through the people who had contributed to its making. Through this crucial route I was restored to my own country's past and to what later would become my pioneering province in the history of Australia's science.

'You always seem to land on your feet', said a long-standing colleague to me recently, if a trifle darkly. And it was true. After four years of *Dictionary* commitment (of which I write in *Breakfast with Beaverbrook*), I had the good fortune to benefit from the influence of two powerful men who were instrumental in propelling me towards a significantly untrodden field.

In 1962 little had been done in Australia on the history of science in this country. Indeed, Australian historians, plunging in different directions, had conspicuously shied away from that sector of intellectual history that touched science and technology. Only Geoffrey Blainey, then an independent historian, was illuminating the history of mining with his lucid studies. Yet it was catching the wind overseas. During 1959 C. P. Snow, both a novelist and a scientist, had published his important book *The Two Cultures*. In which, with his foot in both camps, he had dwelt on the 'polar divide' that had arisen since World War II, separating the humanities and the sciences – a division he saw as dangerous to Western society. Responding to the challenge, British and

American historians were already examining the life of science and had begun gathering the informal manuscript records of scientific men and their societies as a bountiful source for a new discipline.

In Australia, Snow's concept had lodged firmly in the mind of two eminent men, Hancock and Sir John Eccles. Hancock had returned to Australia from Britain in 1957 to direct the Research School of Social Sciences at the Australian National University and the neuroscientist John Eccles, a future Nobel prizeman, was then President of the Australian Academy of Science. This visionary pair saw the importance of blending the 'two cultures' in Australia. In 1962 they appointed me to build a bridge between the History Department of the Research School of Social Sciences at ANU and the Academy of Science. There I was to establish a special archive of informal scientific manuscripts under the Academy's dome and open up the study of Australia's scientific past.

What a gift! Such a chance delivered on a platter to someone untrained in science would never happen in today's competitive professional world. But I was in, and for much of my historian's life I have been immersed in the vivid world of natural history in the nineteenth century and its extending professionalism into the twentieth. From settlers to scientists I came! The word 'scientist' had only become part of the English lexicon in 1833, and would for me embrace that diversely talented and adventurous cavalcade of botanists, naturalists, geologists, zoologists, natural history illustrators, collectors, explorers, surveyors, meteorologists, astronomers and the physical scientists who, drawn by news of the 'fifth continent', had crossed the world to record the wonders of an unexplored land.

With such a privilege, how should I begin? Who would guide me? They were challenging and exciting questions. I turned first to the National Library of Australia and laid the groundwork by building bibliographies of relevant books and papers – written mainly, up till then, by involved scientists. I published these in a series of papers in *Search*, the Journal of the Australian and New Zealand Association for the Advancement of Science (ANZAAS). I then made a survey of the manuscript collections of naturalists and scientific investigators who had either come to settle in Australia, or who had visited it as members of the early British surveys. These had been assiduously gathered in our National and State libraries and museums and I published my survey with the ANU Press as *A Guide to the Manuscript Records of Australian Science*, in 1966. This benchmark work turned out to be especially important as it offered a foundation source for all further study in this rich and untapped field. It also offered convincing proof of the foresight that Australia's librarians had shown in securing for posterity these resources of Australia's scientific heritage.

Australia's first export commodity, it is said, was its natural history. And from the very first days of settlement, specimens of the newly settled country's unique creatures – its insects, flora and fauna, and particularly its vividly coloured birds – were being preserved and packed off by ships to England to stir a lively interest in this astonishing land. It was a time too, emerging from the mid-eighteenth century, when European naturalists were increasingly concerned with establishing order in their understanding of the natural world and with careful systems of taxonomy in which the Linnaean system of classification – with its simple, stable hierarchical divisions into classes, orders, genera and species – held pride of place. Yet, as one British botanist and collector Sir James Smith had noted with awe in 1793: 'When a botanist first enters so remote a country as New Holland, he finds himself in a new world. He can scarcely meet with any fixed points from whence to draw his analogies'. It was even more confounding in the animal kingdom. With its long geological isolation from the rest of the world, Australia had provided a retreat for what appeared to be 'the bizarre and the unrecognizable' marsupials now long extinct in other regions of the earth, as well as other of the most primitive forms of faunal life.

Hence it fell to me to indentify the major participants in the discovery and despatch of these rarities, together with the decipherers of the country's geological structures, its weather and its heavens. In so doing, I would trace the processes that shaped the connections and interrelationship between the colonial investigators and scientists at British and European centres of research. The records of these creative days – the libraries' documentary sources of private letters, journals and diaries – were on hand, and their very rawness caught at the excitement, struggle, exhilaration, frustration and achievement of those pioneering days and marked the private expression and involvement of working science.

The nineteenth century was destined to become one of the great centuries of scientific advance. From massive accumulations of data from around the world, fundamental changes were taking place in the biological and geological sciences; the theory of the evolution and geographical distribution of species (bruited in varied forms) was transforming man's understanding of the very nature of species, while the sciences of astronomy and geography and their related disciplines of meteorology, hydrology, cartography and anthropology were advancing from British, French and American maritime voyages of survey and scientific enquiry.

In this transformation, Australia played a crucial part. Very rapidly after settlement it was visited by French expeditions of discovery. The comte de Lapérouse appeared in Sydney in February 1788; Bruni d'Entrecasteaux called at Van Diemen's Land in 1793; while Nicolas Baudin's grandly equipped expedition, with its large contingent of scientists, reached Australian shores between 1802 and 1804. From this last expedition, important cartographical and natural-history records and an abundant haul of faunal and floral specimens were carried back to France.

Much enlightened and drawing on my *Guide to the Manuscript Record of Australian Science*, I published *Scientists in Nineteenth Century Australia: A documentary history* in 1976. My participants were a lively assortment of botanists, zoologists, geologists, astronomers, surveyors, meteorologists, explorers, inventors and naval officers pushing out the contours and disciplines of science in Australia. Sir Joseph Banks, the adventurous young man who had travelled with Cook on the *Endeavour* to locate the Great South Land, had matured into the powerful botanical supremo, dominating Australia's botanical progress from his seats as President of the Royal Society of London and Director of the Royal Gardens at Kew for the first thirty years. Sending his last communication to the botanical explorer Allen Cunningham in 1820, the year he died, his words had a signature tune:

'I have received safe and in good condition the numerous things you have sent me', he wrote, 'and the Royal Gardens have materially benefitted by what we have had from you. I give you great credit for having for the second time volunteered to go with Captain King [Phillip Parker King] to the north coast, we could have no account of the plants he meets with from any other quarter. I trust and hope, however, you will not be called away any more, but will be able to attend to the inland excursions made from Sydney. I write you a short letter, because I am not well. I know of nothing more to say to you, than that I entirely approve of the whole of your conduct'.

Banks' legacy and influence at Kew Gardens would pass to Sir William Hooker who, as Director, maintained a warm relationship with his Australian collectors. The most notable of these was with Ronald Campbell Gunn, a settler and rising public servant in Van Diemen's Land who, honing his skills as a collecting botanist and systematist, supplied plant specimens for Hooker and his son Joseph Hooker over some forty years.

Adding to the growing knowledge of Australia's natural science was a rising band of London publishers, booksellers and illustrators, while authors and magazine and journal editors played an important role in stimulating a keen public interest in the curious findings from overseas. John Gilbert was the most able of the early naturalist-collectors in Australia. He was brought here in 1838 by his employer John Gould as his key collector, gathering specimens for his employer's masterly books on Australian birds and mammals. As such, Gilbert served in the field from 1838 to 1845, vastly extending the range of materials for the entrepreneurial Gould in London. Here he eagerly communicates to Gould from Western Australia in September 1839:

'Since I last wrote I have increased my collection to 150 Species of Birds; 13 Species of Quadrupeds; about 70 Skeletons; 7 Bottles of Reptiles; etc; a few Fish; 500 Insects; 400 Shells, a few Crustacea, and 3 or 4 hundred Plants ... I have been in the interior as far as any Europeans have yet settled, but unfortunately at the time I was there, the Natives committed several frightful murders on the white people, who to punish them killed several of the Blacks...I was therefore obliged to work myself in the best way I could, but although my efforts were curtailed in this respect I still succeeded in obtaining many Birds not found at Perth'.

Gilbert's communication was prophetic, for he himself fell victim to an Aborigine's spear on his travels as naturalist with Ludwig Leichhardt's overland expedition from eastern Australia to Port Essington in 1845. Colonial scientists also faced marked and enduring challenges in Australia. Twelve-thousand miles away from the comparative suites of specimen at the metropolitan centres of science, and, their local museums slow to grow, they were obliged to send the best of their collections for identification and classification by experts abroad and determinedly build communication links with contacts who could assist them. Leichhardt's recognition of this problem was explicit. Writing to London's pre-eminent palaeontologist, Richard Owen, in 1844, he declared:

'I am desirous of riveting my name more deeply in your memory, and in order to do so, I take the liberty of sending one or two specimens of the collection of fossil bones I made in Darling Downs. It is the young animal of the gigantic Pachyderm, which once lived near and in the swamps and lagoons, which must have covered these rich plain. Is it not curious that a great number of Australian animals, very different in the formation of the body, have a certain resemblance in the lower jaw, and particularly in the two horizontal incisors? I would call it the Australian type, and should say that the large fossil jaw was formed on the same plan on which that of the Kangaroo, of the Opossum, of the Flying squirrel of the Colonists, and of the Koala, is formed without pretending that the animal to which it belonged was either a gigantic Kangaroo or a gigantic Opossum'.

It was a practice that inevitably strengthened the hegemony of northern hemisphere pundits over their colonial colleagues. There were other hazards. By no means all ships carrying colonial correspondence and specimens got through; records of shipwrecks mounted, and the protracted delay between the despatch of precious collections and the long return sea voyage contributed to a dependency on the part of colonial scientists on the knowledge and co-operation of authorities elsewhere. Frustration underwrote their often indefatigable labour. Nonetheless, as the century advanced colonial scientists, shored up by their long researches and local expertise, were eager to move from mere collection and reportage and enter the debate on aspects of theory emanating from the scientific metropolises. In Victoria, the Government botanist and director of the Victorian Botanic Gardens, Ferdinand von Mueller, cherished the hope from his many excursions that he would be chosen to prepare the planned 'Flora of Australia'. To his chagrin, the choice went to the eminent British botanist George Bentham, at Kew.

'I wished it was possible for me' (Mueller wrote the victor in 1862), 'to conduct you for only one walk around some parts of our "bush" and you would fully concur in the limits I have generally assigned to our species... With the profound respect which I entertain for your long experience and maturer judgment, I cannot help to differ from you in the sentiments which you so seriously express in reference to the *non-fixity* of species. I think I had in Australia, where physical conditions are more widely different within limited space than perhaps in most parts of the globe, an opportunity to study the laws of variation of species more carefully in the field & under the most varied circumstances than most other Botanists. And the result of the investigation has *invariably been that species are permanent & immutable*, but that they are subject to vastly more variations than we are accustomed to suppose. They never pass into each other and their weak hybrid offerings nature has designed for speedy destruction in most cases'.

Mueller, as it happened, was wrong. Yet, a committed anti-evolutionist, he considered it 'a duty which I owe to science that I should not withhold my views on this all important question which agitates the naturalists of the day'.

And so the conversations went. I loved drawing upon this active fraternity and plucked extracts of their correspondence to focus the changing environment of science. From the 1830s to the 1850s the future young evolutionists Charles Darwin, Joseph Hooker and Thomas Huxley – those 'co-circum wanderers and fellow labourers' as Darwin later dubbed them – all visited Australian shores as naturalists to the British survey ships (Darwin aboard the HMS *Beagle*, 1836, Hooker with *Erebus* in 1842 and Huxley on *Rattlesnake*, 1846–45) and their Australian experience critically influenced their emergence as the evolutionary action group in Britain. How modern they were! 'I will leave my mark somewhere and it shall be clear and distinct', declared young Huxley. It was. The letter he wrote to his friend, the naturalist W. S. Macleay in Sydney, on his return to London in 1850 significantly reveals one option that was fortunately denied him:

> 'As you *wont* have a Professor of Natural History at Sydney – to my great sorrow I have gone in as a candidate for a Professorial chair at the other end of the world... Had the Sydney University been carried out as originally proposed,

I should certainly have become a candidate for the Natural History Chair'.

Much important and far-reaching work has now been written on these vital visitors and on the large spectrum of early botanists and naturalists in Australia. But, preparing my *Documents* in the late 1960s, I was a lone pioneering researcher in this field. Working on them in the course of my husband's appointment to the United States, I grasped the opportunity of flying to Britain to spend time among the famous botanical collections at Kew. Discussing my proposed documentary volume in London with that remarkable librarian Phyllis Mander Jones, herself then pioneering Australia's Joint Copying Project of Australian Material in Britain, it gave me great encouragement when she exclaimed: 'From Joseph Banks to Lawrence Hargrave and flight technology. What a girth!' It was true. Moreover, the documents contained within them the critical story of the transition from the pursuit of science as an independent activity in Australia to its professional growth and development via the advent of science in the colonial universities.

My *Scientists in Nineteenth Century Australia. A documentary history* drew welcome scholarly praise. Eager to bring this rich cast of characters to a public audience, I followed it with an illustrated book, *'A Bright & Savage Land'. Scientists in Colonial Australia* (1986). And here I could focus on a key component of nineteenth-century science, the natural history illustrators, and reveal the brilliantly coloured landscape of the colonial scientific world: Sydney Parkinson's delicate watercolours of Australian plants; Ferdinand Bauer's evocative-yet-scientifically precise fauna and flora sketched during Flinders' circumnavigation of Australia in 1801–04; and the glowing depictions of Australian animals and silky marine life made by Alexandre Lesueur during Nicolas Baudin's expedition to 'Terra Australis'; and on to Gould. All these illustrations gleamed vividly from the pages together with black-and-white images of fossils, extinct marsupials, land and seascapes, and scientific instruments, which together conveyed a graphically striking picture of scientific activity at the far end of the globe.

'Why did we never think of that?' exclaimed Robyn Williams when *A Bright & Savage Land* appeared. He called it an 'enthralling book' and was generous in his assessing words. 'Nothing', he wrote, 'can convey the gorgeous presentation, the famous pictures of kangaroos, fish, flowers, and such like from the historical archives, and the paintings of the famous cast. They are all there in coffee-table style, but the design also places neat illustrations in the margins with text to match, so that the book can be used on several levels: to skim and admire; to select and focus; or, indeed, to read right through and be edified by Moyal's considerable achievements as a historian of Australian science'.

The contribution of Mead and Beckett, the Macquarie Street publishing partner, to the book's presentation also stirred academic praise. Noting the 'visual and verbal dimensions of historical scholarship', Wade Chambers, a member of the Social Studies in Science program at Deakin University, affirmed that the publisher and I 'must be thanked for an example of Australian bookmaking' – 'hundreds of illustrations, not one lacking in interest and 77 in full colour'. Although he took me to rightful task for my lack of bibliographic or iconographic details for the illustrations (and I trust I learnt from him); I cheered his recognition that my attempt to reveal Australian science was not carried out in isolation, but alive to the social and intellectual context in which it grew. 'Read in this spirit', Chambers, a member of an advancing corps of contributors to the history of science summed up, 'I found Ann Moyal's book both interesting, long overdue, and an aesthetic joy'.

'The dead need history', wrote the historian Greg Dening as Max Crawford Professor of History at the University of Melbourne. But we need them keenly too. Those gallant, enquiring men were my continuing cohort and companions and a source of much delight. Indeed, as the 'istors' plunges into their subject's context their influence and their probing minds, they often become more alive to them than their contemporaries.

CHAPTER 3

THE YELLOW RUG.
THE STORY OF A MARRIAGE.

Along with my passion for history, I had been married to Joe Moyal for more than thirty years. We had come together from the far ends of the earth. While a paper in the *New Scientist* examining how humans choose their mate had revealed, surprisingly, that the average distance between the birth place of a husband and wife and where they married was a mere 177 kilometres, Joe was born in 1910 in Jerusalem in the then bare, stretching country of Palestine and I had arrived some sixteen years later 12,000 miles away in Sydney. We met in Canberra at University House in 1958.

Since Palestine had long been part of the Ottoman Empire until Turkey's wartime defeat in 1918 opened the vast Empire to diplomatic dispersal, Jose Enrique Moyal, as he was named, was nominally both a Palestinian and a Turk. Joe was the only child of an eccentric but well-reputed Jewish lawyer and a quietly reserved French teacher who had come to Palestine with her father, an Inspector of Schools. His merchant grandfather had cultivated close relations with the Turkish authorities and was made a Bey. Joe's mother had abandoned him and the small family when he was four for a second marriage to a Greek doctor and Joe had been reared by a largely absentee father and Arab servants in the then small town of Tel Aviv, where he attended the local Gymnasium. From there, being gifted though un-mentored, he had made his way to Cambridge, and to further education and postgraduate studies in France where he trained as an electrical engineer. But it was science that drew him back to Paris in the late 1930s where he gained his knowledge of mathematical statistics and theoretical physics.

As the Germans descended on Paris in June 1940, Joe escaped to Britain and, now a British citizen of the Palestine Mandate, had spent the war serving as an electrical engineer and research mathematician at the de Havilland Aircraft Company. After the war he became an academic and, acquiring considerable reputation in mathematics at Manchester University, came to the Australian National University as Reader in Statistics in 1958. When in November that year I arrived at the ANU at University House, the 'Oxbridge college in the bush', the bespectacled, glossy-dark-haired Joe Moyal stood out among the residents – a sophisticated man widely read in history and philosophy as few scientists were. With his deep, faintly accented voice, a mind betrothed to thought, and a jaunty knack on the dance floor, he drew me in and, freed from our respective cycles of divorce, we married early in 1963.

In my earlier memoir I wrote briefly of our marriage. 'We enjoyed a great affinity, and in our differing ways, nourished and stimulated each other. Loving, good talk, a rich intellectual life, protection and support, journeyings and lovely places, encouragement for me in all I did, yielded a fulfilling diet'. Our first married years we spent in Canberra, where I embraced my new profession in the history of science and Joe became an influential figure, training the postgraduates who would later fill the chairs of mathematics and statistics in the growing Australian universities. Late in 1964, however, he was headhunted by America's leading laboratory – Argonne National Laboratory near Chicago – and I, well aware after my short-lived British ventures, that this marriage must succeed, packed up my research cargo of nineteenth-century naturalists and carried them, not entirely willing immigrants, to the frozen winter reaches of Illinois.

'The town is beastly', snapped Bertram Russell, 'and the weather vile'. And it was in that first fierce winter – when sleet and snow bore down on 'the windy city' and our resort apartment near Argonne gave off its deep silences – that we found close dependence on each other and, celebrating, bought a finely woven pale-yellow rug which became our talisman of comfort and love.

With my Australian documentary history of science as my companion, for a time I also took up an appointment as science editor at the renowned University of Chicago Press. But we both found that while we loved the expansive life of art and music in Chicago and the intellectual contacts offered by that city's great university, we recoiled from the long conflict of the Vietnam war, the assassinations, on the cusp of change, of Martin Luther King and Robert Kennedy, and the encroaching management of control that penetrated the universities and scientific institutions. On being offered an academic post in Sydney in 1971, I chose to leave while Joe waited one year more before he took up his final professorship at Sydney's Macquarie University.

Can one describe a marriage; it is made of so many parts? We were often in different places, I in Brisbane for two years in the late seventies as director of the Science Policy Research Centre at Griffith University, and Joe finishing his influential teaching and research career in mathematics at Macquarie University where the Head of Department observed 'We found we had a giant among us'. But we exulted in our vivid holidays together snorkelling on the Great Barrier Reef. In 1980 we came together in a

Canberra townhouse where I wrote *Clear Across Australia*, my all embracing history of telecommunications commissioned by Telecom Australia, and Joe was my enthusiastic, supporting friend.

Yet I long knew that I had married what Patrick White called 'a burnt one'. A rejected child from a broken and unloving home, he carried the affliction of depression and could be a great rejecter himself. I kept a foot for research in our Sydney flat, independence my solution, but in all those periods of disjunction I thought of him always as the most civilized of men, generous and courteous, adventurous and with a deeply retentive and ranging mind. In 1991, I sold the Sydney flat and returned to live permanently in Canberra. We adopted then the habit, common among British literary couples and clearly envied by some Canberra friends, of living in separate townhouses a short walking distance from each other.

Friends came. Joe's cousin, Schemuel Moyal, distinguished limb of his Jewish Israeli family of judges and diplomats, arrived in Canberra in 1995 as the Israeli Ambassador with Nora his musician wife, bringing family resemblances and old memories. My sister, Mimi, and her long time companion Judith were constant visitors. They sat at Joe's feet relishing his informed conversation, deep in their attachment, joining in picnics, dinners and excursions. Retired from teaching, he plied his mathematician's craft, 'incubating' concepts, engaged, original, but less given now to writing up his ideas. He was also a film buff, a wine connoisseur, a man of history, art and politics, and an ever-ready dipstick for me into scientific and technological ideas. I called him 'my fertile friend'. I was glad that I had made my life with him.

Joe turned eighty in 1990. 'I never thought I'd be old', he told me surprised one day. Younger by sixteen years, does one notice a significant age divide only when it takes clear form? But, remembering his enjoyment of a cigar in middle years, sly emphysema assailed him, and he moved in and out of hospital as the decade progressed. Then it was that he would come to convalesce in my townhouse wrapped in the yellow rug, the talisman, cosy in the sitting room's sunshine, a book in hand. In hospital again in June 1995, he could not attend the launch of *Breakfast with Beaverbrook*, but I found him being shunted by trolley for tests around the clinical corridors clutching the book. Restored for periods we would go out to lunch or dine, to the National Art Gallery with its windowed glimpses of the lake, and spend our evenings together. By day, an efficient young woman came to cook and clean for him. It was a time of closeness, but I feared the inevitable aloneness that must come.

Yet in all our years together, one thing was noteworthy: Joe rarely spoke of his children. He had arrived in Canberra from Manchester University, divorced or divorcing. And with his departure to his tenured post in Australia, his German-born Jewish wife had moved to San Francisco with their twenty-two-year-old daughter and their teenage son to open a Jewish retirement home. I would meet his daughter married to an American lawyer and the mother of twin boys, and his son a student at Antioch University, when we arrived in America in 1965. Yet our meetings were rare. Neither Joe nor I ever encountered his former wife. Indeed it appeared as if that whole period from his marriage from 1935 until the mid-'50s had been virtually eclipsed. It also seemed that Joe, himself a rejected child, had emotionally divested himself of his growing and already grown children, just as his mother before him had, in his extreme childhood, divested him.

But as his health waned in the early '90s, might he not, I thought, enjoy being in touch with them again. Proud of this idea,

I took the initiative to restore contact with his daughter and for Joe to send kind messages to his former wife whom, we learnt, was suffering from cancer. But my plan for us to meet his children for a holiday at the Barrier Reef faltered when his daughter withdrew at the eleventh hour and, holidaying with his son, I quickly found that, he was more concerned with having an adventurous time with his young American wife than spending time with his father. Yet he was not un-resourceful, for I soon received a letter from Joe's solicitor telling me that while Joe's Will had not changed, there had been 'very substantial changes to the assets'.

As Joe's illnesses deepened, I sent a letter to his daughter in June 1995. 'He has had a bad time lately', I wrote. 'Seven weeks ago he entered hospital with chronic blocked airway disease, whisked off by ambulance when staying with me. A specialist established some control during his sixteen days in hospital, and he came home to me complete with Nebulizer and various drugs and slowly worked his way back to mobility. But ten days ago he began haemorrhaging heavily and returned to hospital, his blood count very low. His legs are full of fluid from long swelling from the lymph gland operation he had in the '80s and tests revealed that the fluid had markedly affected his lungs and heart. He would, I felt sure, appreciate hearing from her'.

These days in hospital were challenging for Joe and I would sit beside him for many hours, taking my work with me, at that time a mass of the scientific correspondence of Australia's pioneering geologist the Rev. W. B. Clarke. 'How is Mr Clarke?' he would ask each day as I settled beside him with my spilling folders. But we were together and his specialist had called me aside to say that his condition was steadily deteriorating and that age and multiple problems were bearing down on him. Yet valiant by temperament and future-oriented, Joe came home again. Events would shape in June 1996.

Once more sharp illness struck and Joe was back in hospital, pale and ill, with a negative prospect for his future and quality of life. Schemuel and Nora Moyal, loving and attentive, visited plainly saddened by what old age can do. 'Joe looks at you with love', said Nora. And again he came home, this time to his own house where, at his most fragile, I kept him company. Perhaps he was in touch with his children or they with him, for on 27 June, with brief brisk notice, his daughter arrived from the United States. Since I could not leave him to meet her, I sent a welcoming message to the airport.

'Get out: I'm in charge', were the striking words which this commanding woman, dressed in black, hurled at me at Joe's front door. 'Show me your papers'! What? I was incredulous! When, in the face of Joe's forlorn cry, 'I'm not strong enough to cope', I withdrew to return with food supplies for him the next morning, his apartment locks had been changed and, knocking to enter, I was instantly handed a letter from his solicitor that banned any further contact. Several days later I confronted the daughter's plan with her solicitor for a 'Dissolution of Marriage' document.

Pain and shock leap from the entries in my diary of those extraordinary days. Could this actually be happening? Yet it became evident that Joe's daughter, married to a San Francisco lawyer and herself a forceful former administrator of the U.S. protectorate of Guam, had arrived with careful preparation and premeditation. Caught in such bizarre circumstances I was blown off course. Ambushed, yet confident as a wife of my protected rights, I began to pour over legal documents that could shed light on the situation where a husband and wife had different residences.

In Australian law there appeared to be no protection. Indeed I was to discover that, while 'de factos' of every kind dwelling with a partner were well protected in their legal rights, there was no legal provision in 1996 for a wife who did not share the communal home.

'How' asked horrified friends, 'can a non-citizen come in from America and use Australian law against you, unprotected?' It was a good question. I consulted a long established Canberra legal firm. Clearly surprised by the unnatural situation, the question appeared to turn on the condition of Joe's mind – too ill to cope – or whether we were dealing with 'betrayal' or 'duress'. I gave my lawyer a copy of *Breakfast with Beaverbrook* to convey the background of our lives, a Trojan horse. Her recommendation was the Community Advocate.

Extruded, I fell into a continuous ricocheting flu, dragging myself about my house, trying, as writers do, to make my way through confronting times by working. There were terrible interruptions. 'Three times today', I noted in my diary on July 23, 'the old woman with flying white hair has knocked on my front door to deliver Divorce Papers'. Did all solicitors employ old women for the wily delivery of such threatening mail? An invisible vantage point at my bedroom window protected me. Whatever malice was I dealing with? I would soon learn. The Community Advocate employed to determine the state of Joe's mind had been at pains to tell me after our telephone discussion that he had carefully taken down my account of the situation and would now visit Joe and interview him alone. In the event, Joe was closely attended by his daughter. There was another element in the story. These two family members, father and daughter, had not spent time together for almost forty years and Joe's guilt at leaving the domestic home had perhaps lain deep below the surface. Fragile now and near to death, it was a time for bonding. Her constant presence and his need for assurance and attention were crucial factors. While the Community Advocate had reported to my solicitor that 'Joe was sound in mind though vulnerable', no further action ensued. I remained outside the ring.

Marooned, I drew support from friends. I met my sister Mimi and Judy, in Sydney that July. Mimi had loved Joe dearly for many years yet now, she said, she had come to 'hate that old man'. She had tried, along with other friends, to speak to him by telephone. Impossible. He was reported as either 'asleep', 'had just gone out', 'was resting' or 'busy'. He remained firmly isolated from the outside world. When at length, she gained his ear, he said. 'All is all right here. My daughter is looking after me'.

The warmth of close friends strengthened me. We underrate their value in our lives. Constant and caring, for they had known me in my marriage since 1963, they kept me sane company. Arriving home one afternoon, a brilliant bunch of flowers sat on my doorstep with a note from my English friend Maureen, in London, who had spent several months with Joe and me years earlier in Canberra. 'Writing', it read, 'but still reeling!'. Mimi and my old friend Lorna Howlett were busy writing affidavits which testified to my sustained care and nursing of Joe over the past six years – how astonishing that we had to write it down – while Schemuel and Nora Moyal declined all pressing invitations from Joe's daughter to call.

Neighbours shed light. Joe's daughter and her husband, newly arrived from America, had disappeared and Joe was 'staying with friends' (for which read, 'put into a Nursing Home'). By September, they had returned to the United States and Joe was now permanently installed in a small room in an establishment for the aged in a suburb neighbouring my own. But strict instructions had been issued that I was to have no access. One morning, however, my bright cousin Judy and I made a daring entry and found Joe in bed in considerable bleakness and disarray. Photographs of his first wife, his children, his grandchildren and great grandchildren decked the shelves. He rose, his poor face twitching. 'You were a terrible wife', he said. 'Come away', said my cousin kindly.

They offered me $1,800, but I fought the divorce and found reprieve in a sympathetic woman judge.

My life resumed. My work, that ever present routine, went on. Yet there was my husband of more than three decades of whom I had written in my autobiography two years before, 'Across my life of scholarship and action, I know one thing: the thread that has made it buoyant and persistent is a complex and lasting love'. Now his townhouse was put to market, his fine scientific library promised elsewhere, profitably sold, and he himself cast into a room in a retirement village. Marked as 'No access', I could sometimes manage to slip into the 'village' at night when staff were occupied in their duties and talk to him, the old Joe, calm now, and happy to see me. In 1997 I helped him purchase a small unit in the same establishment and furnish it with his familiar things.

But his life was moving towards its close. It was a slender reed with many buffeting winds. He was intermittently in and out of hospital. 'I am not afraid of death', he told me, 'I have had so many illnesses, I would not mind it'. I knew him well and was often at his side. He still took a keen interest in Israel, 'that eyelash of land around the Mediterranean shore'. Late in 1996 he had enjoyed the pleasure of being awarded an honorary Doctorate of Letters by the ANU for his singular contribution to the three fields of mathematics, statistics and physics – a valued and confirming act. His large daughter, robed, sat behind him on the platform. I sat hidden in the crowded hall. But early in 1998 he received papers from American scientists that made crucial use of work which he had first defined in a pioneering paper on a 'Statistical Basis for Quantum Physics' in 1949. It was a paper that would reverberate beyond his lifetime, through many disciplines, as the old century moved to the new.

Life, however, delivers its own timing. Long committed to go for a carefully organised holiday in Indonesia in the middle of April 1998, I learnt at the airport that Joe had been taken to Canberra Hospital the previous night suffering from a slight stroke. Again I was debarred on 'family instructions' from personal telephone contact. But a carer from the retirement village consoled me: 'Joe is very strong', she said, 'he will make sure that he is here when you get back'. The days, however, darkened. Staying with new friends in Jakarta they succoured me in ways that marked them forever in my heart. But Joe's condition worsened, a tube was inserted in his throat: it seemed that he would die. How cruel that this should happen while I was far away. Pretending to be my friend Lorna, I got through to the hospital and asked the nurse to put the telephone to his ear. I spoke into its silence telling him that I loved him and thought of him always. I wept in his ear. He improved slightly and two days later I could speak to him again. 'I love you', I said. 'Mutual', came the distant, familiar, faint reply.

A day later I am ringing from a public phone in Ubud, and he tells me: 'They have saved my life, but I need help'. 'What help?' I ask. 'To hold my hand. I'm hanging on here', he says, his voice now audible, 'I'd like to see you'. I arrive at last on May 3rd. Encased in the room for the very sick behind the nurse's counter, lean and clean, his hair still glossy brown but tinged with white, he says, 'I'm dying but I've been hanging on for you. I love you Ann. You are the love of my life'.

'Death is so irreversible', he adds, 'I wanted to hang on to tell you that I love you'.

And so for three weeks we fell into our old accustomed bonded ways, no longer an old man, his long fine hands, his dark-rimmed spectacles, so distinguished a look. I take him the light yellow rug from his little flat. I also take him the richly bound *honoris causa* award from the ANU of which he is justly proud. 'I am not one of the crowd', he observes quietly. On May 8th, his solicitor, prevaricating, reluctant, gives me Enduring Power of Attorney. Joe is very clear now. 'I am guilty to have put this upon you', he says, 'but I love you'. His mind expansive, recalling Deuteronomy; he alludes to 'The Children of Lot' (those children, who, 'received land and possession which could not then be given to anyone else'). 'They were wicked, my children', he says quietly. 'I have been converted, I love you'. But there is little escape from the enveloping pain. *'Aidez-moi, Dieu'*, he calls in the familiar language of his boyhood. His children do not come. Morphine at last arrives. At times, he gives me his small squarish smile. 'My dear heart', I call him gently all that week. The doctor calls him Lazarus; but not this time. 'Shalom and Peace', I say to him when I depart that early evening of 22 May 1998. The leaves fold. Two hours later a Sister rings to tell me, 'Professor Moyal died two hours ago'.

We assemble together, so small a party, at the Crematorium: my sister, Mimi, Schemuel and Nora Moyal, a carer from the retirement village, my Uniting Church clergyman friend David Webster, who has managed to wrest Joe's body from the funeral home, his wife my old friend Hilary, and the village padre. Ambassador Moyal, cap on head, commits Joe's body in Hebrew and English, his link to his homeland marked. David Webster and the padre say their gentle familiar prayers. It is a triumph and an ending. He had passed from my life and I will long grieve for him.

The following year of 1999, I laid the foundation for the J. E. Moyal Lecture and Medal at Macquarie University where Joe spent his last professional years. There, circling sequentially, an outstanding statistician, a mathematician, and a physicist receive the annual award which grows in renown and stature every year.

CHAPTER 4

GENESIS. THE INDEPENDENT SCHOLARS ASSOCIATION OF AUSTRALIA

Those years of the 1990s, tangled and saddening in my personal life as they became, were also open widely to new ideas. Early in the decade my mind had swung to a question I'd thought about since leaving academia in 1980 and which I'd touched on briefly in the last pages of *Breakfast with Beaverbrook*. 'We have too small an intelligentsia in Australia', I wrote there. 'We have, too, an unhealthy dependence on a handful of visible pundits and discussants. We lack the vigorous intellectual criticism that can so richly characterise British, French and American public life. I believe the time is ripe to consider an 'Academy of Independent Scholars' in Australia for the formation not of an 'invisible college', but of an 'alternative' college, for the assembling of distinguished and promising independent thinkers who, working outside institutions and the established academies, can offer an open and diverse critique'. It was now clearly time to move on.

Since I had resigned from Griffith University in some disgust early in 1980, it had taken some time to grasp the nature of the independence created by leaving tenured academia. I had accepted Telecom Australia's offer to write its history – which became my magnum opus *Clear Across Australia* – with interest and relief and completing this demanding task in two-and-a-half brisk years, I was able to invest some part of its remuneration as a basis for further research. I also had the good fortune (at least for a non-university-based researcher), to win one or two small Australian Research Council (ARC) grants. But while sundered from academic funding in a tenured post, I was soon to find that I had by no means left universities behind. I was invited to spend periods as an honorary Visiting Fellow in several university departments – in government at Sydney University, in economics at the University of Queensland, in history and later economic-history at the ANU, and in Media Studies at Macquarie University. And so I continued to perform as an academic scholar, publishing papers, churning out conference papers, writing in different fields for the media, reviewing theses by invitation, and serving as founding honorary editor of the new telecommunication-and-science-policy journal *Prometheus*, all activities that were tasks of an appointed academic career. Yet, increasingly in my heart (and certainly in my purse), I grew to recognise that I was outside the system, an independent, albeit with some rueful satisfaction in going 'against the grain'.

I knew that independent scholarship was a tradition that stretched back to Greek and medieval times. And in later centuries, great independent thinkers had worked outside the ivory towers: Charles Darwin tellingly styled his great scientific labours 'in silence and solitude'. By the 1990s in Australia pertinent influences were also at work. As constraints and contractions grew in the university sector, there was a gathering stream of scholars eager to take early retirement and conduct their scholarly investigations beyond the academic halls.

When, then, in 1993, I was invited to join the committee of Canberra's Centre for Australian Cultural Studies – run by the lively social historian David Headon and which also held Patricia Clarke, author of many books on Australia's early literary women – I put forward the idea of forming an association of independent scholars and won their instant support. We agreed that there was already a diverse body of thinkers and writers whose expertise spread over wide fields of our national culture, in history, literature, politics, sociology, the arts, regional and international relationships, science and technology to name a few, but who, through isolation and scattered presence were nationally less valued than they ought to be. To frame an association to harness such scholars was an exciting thought and we were soon on the march.

I enlisted the interest and generous assistance of that great powerhouse for independent scholars the National Library of Australia, where Warren Horton, director and powerful supremo, immediately seized on the relevant interconnections for the Library of an Independent Scholars plan. He granted a thousand dollars annually and the free use of the Library's conference room for the organisation's inaugural meeting, a generous gift that has continued through successive directors to the present day. A participant group had also come together to define the association's character and goals: Pat Clarke and David Headon, literary writer and bibliographer Joy Hooton, cultural critic Humphrey McQueen, historians John Moses and Margaret Stevens – all sources of fertile thinking who offered congenial company. Margaret Stevens, attached to the *Australian Dictionary of Biography* but also working on her own research, had written to me after reading *Breakfast with Beaverbrook*, 'I was a few paces there behind you – and waving!' Now she became a ready sounding board. A growing number of us were on our way together.

We called the first conference of our new association 'Against the Grain' and, from the one-hundred-strong participants who arrived from all over the country to attend its sessions at the National Library in August 1995, the 'Independent Scholars Association of Australia' was born. It was a happy coincidence that one of Australia's outstanding independent intellectuals Nugget Coombs, had noted in a recent ABC Radio broadcast what he saw as 'a declining moral dimension of the intelligentsia' and argued that the battle of ideas was being won by 'an uncaring corporate society with no sense of community'. 'The intelligentsia', he concluded bleakly, 'have sold out'.

It was a theme for our conference that rang particularly true. Australian universities were then enmeshed in structural change, new pressures were being put on academic staff and, linked with constraints on tenure and pressure to attract grants, there was an evident sense of insecurity among younger and middle academics and a widespread unease among creative thinkers that universities were no longer the bastions of intellectual integrity and freedom of ideas. They stood as compelling reasons for the establishment of an Independent Scholars Association whose purpose was both to serve as a collective community and offer a forum to stimulate informed and independent debate in the public sphere. We were launching, I said in my opening address, 'A Declaration of Independence' at the conference 'what we believe is the first association of its kind in the world'.

Much cheered by the wide response and the welcome media attention we attracted, we set about devising a charter and constitution. A Canberra-based Provisional Council was set up under the aegis of the Centre for Australian Cultural Studies; I accepted the role of President for the first five years. Joy Hooton became Vice-President while Pat Clarke became our nourishing Honorary Secretary. In these formative years formats changed around the goals and strategies which ISAA (as we encoded it) might achieve. But our core purposes stood firm. We set them down in the membership form: 'To raise the profile of independent scholars in Australia and increase awareness of their diversity and expertise; to facilitate the wide contribution of independent scholars to the public sphere; and to provide community and contact for scholars, who, for the most part, conduct their work in circumstances of some isolation. 'Later we would add 'to give a voice to dissent'.

We were fortunate in the participants we attracted. When we held the second ISAA conference 'How Free is Speech?' soon after the General Election of 1996 which returned the Howard Government to power, the eminent Professor of Theology at Melbourne University, Max Charlesworth, a new member, opened it with stirring words: 'The founding of this Association has turned out to be a stroke of genius,' he declared, 'since it now looks that, under the new political regime, there is going to be a reversion to the grey values of the Menzies era. In this climate independent scholarship will be enormously important. The politicisation of the bureaucracy, the nobbling of the universities – though we have to admit that they have, alas, never played a radical critical role in Australian society – the globalisation of the media, the emasculation of the ABC, and the curious attack on what the Prime Minister calls "political correctness" – all these foreboding tendencies', he summed up, 'indicate that free speech and independent thinking are going to need all the friends they can get for the next six years'.

From our first public appearance, ISAA attracted scholars from a wide stream of disciplines with solid achievements in their fields. They included historians, pre-historians, sociologists, theologians, political scientists, anthropologists, science historians, biographers, information economists, scientists, internationalists, writers, film makers, broadcasters, publishers, editors, librarians, media commentators, former diplomats, public servants and scholars of India, Asia and China. As I was always drawn to the very oddness and brave appearance of the boab tree, its branches sprouting from its upturned root bowl, we adopted it as the society's emblem attaching as the leitmotif: 'The boab tree is self-sustaining; it draws on its own resources. Upside down, it flourishes against the grain'.

We were very happy in those shaping years as the new association slid vigorously from one conference or participatory seminar to the next. 'You are always so busy', my husband lamented, and he was right. My diary of those years resounds with notes of devising programs, taking and typing minutes, organising, printing and distributing papers, soliciting and giving press interviews, and writing about ISAA for likely journals. We were building an involved new community and our confidence soared. The distinguished publisher John Iremonger, who joined our ranks, argued persuasively that scholars in Australia and notably the universities, were not reaching out to the community and communicating their works, but were instead talking among themselves. While former-diplomat-turned-academic Alison Broinowski saw in ISAA's annual conferences a pressing need to 'encourage members to be controversial, to rock the boat'.

While ISAA was conceived as apolitical, there was a common advocacy among us that scholarship cannot be quarantined from politics and that abuses of power required enduring scrutiny. And so our annual conferences struck relevant themes. In 1997, when 'downsizing' was ushering in workforce reduction and human change – most conspicuously in the Commonwealth public sector under the determined leadership of the head of the Prime Minister and Cabinet's Department, Max Moore-Wilton – our annual conference on 'Downsizing and the "Contented Society"' drew a large response. There, Professor Sol Encel, Sydney's leading sociologist and early member, adroitly focussed his theme as 'Downsizing, Rightsizing and Capsizing' while Barry Jones, who had alerted hordes of readers to the disappearance of public intellectuals in his *Sleepers' Wake*, expressed his delight at being invited to speak on 'the rising anti-intellectual mood in Australia and the retreat from reason in our politics'.

There would be a continuing stream of published *Conference Proceeding* that pushed ISAA's tentacles out into such controversial contemporary topics, while the *ISAA Review*, initially an in-house journal for members launched early in 1999, became a refereed journal a few years on. Its editor, Dr Gretchen Poiner, underlined 'the richness of ISAA's scholarly ways of seeing and doing, involving exploration, reflection, critique and imagination' while Michael McKernan, prolific military historian and early member, summed up ISAA's membership buoyantly as 'a large common room with the critical rigour of a university-trained membership, but the ability to spot bullshit at fifty paces'!

I was proud of the members we had drawn. Our roll call for the first five years held many distinguished Australians – Don Baker, Veronica Brady, Alison and Richard Broinowski, Max Charlesworth, Patricia Clarke, the scientists Ian Cowan and Doug Cocks, Rosemary Dobson, John Eddy, Meredith Edwards, Sol Encel, Jim and Helga Griffin, Anne Godfrey-Smith, Tom Frame, David Headon, Helen Hewson, Joy Hooton, John Iremonger, Ann-Mari and Joseph Jordens, Anna Lanyon, Marie de Lepervanche, Isabel McBryde, Humphrey McQueen, John Moses, John Mulvaney, David Oldfield, Ros Pesman, John Poynter,

Andrew Reimer, Michael Roe, Anne Summers, Jim Staples, Colin Steele, Susan Steggall, Martin Thomas, Keith Tognetti, Elizabeth Truswell, Judith Wright, and many more.

Our actions were an experiment in organisation. From 1997, individual ISAA chapters took shape in New South Wales, the ACT and Victoria and stretched our opportunities outward. Public communication was critical to us and the advent of Phillip Adams as one of our first members was a striking bonus; the engaged and engaging Phillip gave me generous time each year on 'his little wireless program' 'Late Nite Live' at the ABC to discuss our program – a communication source that reached out widely across Australia. For my part, I rather nobly endured unflattering photographs in interviews with the press (how they love to get under you and take your jaw!). While in 1999 a generous member, an Asia expert based in Singapore, donated finance to enable us to initiate a $15,000 ISAA Book Prize for the best work of independent scholarship published in Australia in each of the two following years.

Across our history we would grapple with that often posed question: what is an 'independent scholar'? Prescriptions came and went. Initially we offered membership 'to those who had a record of published (or for playwrights 'presented') work. We also included those 'Friends of ISAA' who, while in gainful employment, had made a substantial contribution through their profession to knowledge and were in sympathy with the Association's concepts and aims. But the division soon proved conflictive or at least confused, and over time the term melded into a broader, perhaps less elitist, concept of independent scholars – those who were committed to, and interested in, scholarly ideas and critical debate.

For me it had proved a highly creative adventure, full of stimulus and fun. But I believed that a founding parent should take off in good time and I retired from the Presidency in 2001. One of our members Dr Irmgard Heidler, who shared my disciplinary interests in the history of science and had become an active figure in ISAA's Melbourne Chapter while her husband served as head of the Goethe Society in Victoria, became an international voice for the Australian Association on her return to Germany. Writing in her 2002 essay in the *Journal of the American Association of Independent Scholars* (which we found had been formed at almost the same time and with explicitly similar goals to our own) generously summed up: 'Ann Moyal was the motor behind many co-operations, presenting her ideas in numerous papers, providing for the flow of information between organisations and members, and offering encouragement to members. Her most important role seems to have been that of gaining members and keeping them'. I liked it – 'a churning, noisy, five-year motor'. It seemed an apt metaphor!

Certainly the formation of ISAA as an intellectual and cultural agency marked a positive initiative in my career. Organisations of course are built to change. When I passed the President's baton to Sydney member Dr Gretchen Poiner, I remembered her words: 'Ann, it's like letting one of your children go. They grow, change, and you are very proud of them'. Across the years a string of annual conferences and the *ISAA Review* have offered independent scholars opportunities for community and debate; chapters have grown strongly in several States, and there is a varied and enduring company. Many distinguished scholars have remained members of the national body across many years, and diverse others have joined our ranks. I absorb the annual

Members' List and the Association's *Newsletter*; their spread and influence are ranging. 'ISAA', writes one accomplished author and *Newsletter* contributor, 'has been a lifeline for me in retirement'. In a changing world it still has consonance.

It is true that one of ISAA's founding goals (one I have always prized) – to link its membership as articulate players in the public sphere and offer public communication on the Association's behalf – has been abandoned by processes to produce a wider church. But there is evidence that a changing circle of participants is presenting research to a cooperative ISAA community. As a 'mother', I watch it thoughtfully.

CHAPTER 5

A LATE LOVE

My kind of woman lives in the world juggling its opportunities with the need to lead a balanced life. Reading a recent obituary of Margaret Thatcher I came upon a description of her – 'the qualities of self-reliance, diligence, trustworthiness and initiative' that enable someone to live and work independently in society. They are good words and for me resonant words, though I never cared for Mrs Thatcher.

It was in the midst of my trauma with my husband's family that I received a letter from a man I had met briefly almost four decades earlier, when he and his first wife visited University House where I was living. I had given him no thought since. Yet late in 1996, an eclectic reader much drawn to bookshop browsing, he had picked up a copy of my autobiography and, remembering our slight acquaintance, had written, as he lived for most of the year in Canberra, that we might have coffee together. 'By all means', was my reply. A telephone call from him, as I lay in bed felled by flu in those dark days, came a month later, his voice distinctive and chatty, and very cheering to me.

We met for lunch that October in a small suburban restaurant, he a slender man with a nice smile, a ready laugh, a slight deafness, and a faint look of discontent, neatly dressed in a blue seersucker suit. Three hours and much conversation later, the restaurant staff rattled their chairs. 'M.', as I call him, had had a distinguished career, despite his disclaimers, which was unknown to me. Just old enough to go to war in early 1943, he had served on a Royal Australian Navy destroyer around Papua New Guinea and Dutch New Guinea supporting the landings under Douglas MacArthur in 1943–44. From there the war took him to Morotai, into the Leyte Gulf, with a final jump to the main landings in the Philippines which led to the capture of Manila. There the ships' members were able to go ashore and see something of the local life and, at war's end, the *Warramunga* had the distinction of anchoring in Tokyo Bay at MacArthur's signing of the peace treaty with Japan.

Vivid times they were which, for him, had large consequences. Fascinated by what he saw in Manila and realising how little we knew of what was happening in Australia's neighbouring Asian countries, he decided to learn more and, if chance came his way, to shape an academic career that embraced this. This he had done through writing, books, conferences, teaching and the shaping of special centres for his field. He was a specialist in the study of political and social changes in countries that, postwar, had gained their independence from colonial rule – countries which moved at times by violent patterns to strength and power. An Emeritus Professor, at seventy-two M. was still actively and intently absorbed in these engrossing fields.

How delightful it was to have a new friend and one who lifted my mind from my personal confrontation. We took off to a Shakespearian play and a gathering of Friends of the ABC and went our separate way for Christmas. But I soon received a letter telling me of his other house at the Victorian seaside, and how much he would like to show it to me. What odd and striking turns life takes. For our friendship grew. I had told him little of my predicament; yet, slowly, almost stately in its gentle pace, love came, as it does, unexpectedly.

Both M. and I had had three marriages, our lives shaped into our own forms of independent living. When I visited his Canberra home, I noted in my diary, 'his house is very clean, touchingly so. In its way, it's rather beautiful, like him, the Asian bowls and hangings, the new green sheets – the heart turns'. He was handsome, lithe and slim, with a grave face and a sudden soft laugh and smile. I wondered what he looked like as a young man: 'drop-dead handsome' one of his former students was quick to tell me. Walking down a mountain slope, he moved like a ballet dancer. I found this most appealing.

But while there was little doubt that love had entered our arena, there was no thought of marriage. Hearing of a new woman in his life, M.'s eldest son (remembering the many others) had strongly urged against it. And neither of us, with high individuality in our separate lives, wished to acquire a shared permanent residence. I found great happiness in my townhouse, with its high ceilings and little gallery, a study and a spare room for friends who visited, while his quite small home brimmed with shelves of books, with more books and papers on every chair and table – all part of the vast, heaping untidiness of the scholar. Where would I fit? We were, moreover, independent spirits.

M. also, it seemed to me, was a man who had lost confidence in love. From his talk of wives, loves and a 'significant other', I found myself noting early (for a diary is a telling way to chart a love affair) that he was an innately cautious man. Yet in January 1997, dining out at one of our small restaurants, he asks, 'Will we have a relationship?' Coming from an age when it was a proposal of marriage that had tripped lightly off the eager suitor's tongue I had never been asked that question before. 'A relationship', I thought, 'how modern!' So 'yes', I answered, and my new love who, I was sure, would never add to my list of proposals, put a loving and incautious public arm around me.

In the midst of my personal trauma, I felt suddenly, if undeservedly, happy. Love was a great restorative, 'a high: a fix', writes the experienced Doris Lessing. It was also amazingly time-absorbing. I had been re-reading H. G. Wells' famous novel *Ann Veronica*, a habit I indulge from time to time when seeking assurance and calm. For, many decades before the book had become something of a feminist tract, my discerning mother had been reading it as she waited for my birth and chose to name me after its independent-minded heroine. Endowed with this 'postcard from the outside world', it was almost predestined that I would take on some of the characteristics of this rebellious creature, child of a conservative British household in the late nineteenth century who had taken to science, fallen in love with her biology teacher, proclaimed free love, and declared that she 'wanted to take life by the throat'. Taking up her buoyant cry, I had done so.

Now I would respond once more to her telling words. 'The realization that she was in love', Ann Veronica reflected, 'flooded her mind and altered the quality of all its topics. She began to think persistently of Capes [the biology master]. It occurred to her that it was absurd and wrong to be so continuously thinking of one engrossing topic, and she made a strenuous effort to force her mind to other questions'. Wells, a keen pursuer of talented women himself, had got it right. My scholarly concentration fled. Yet loving was also learning. M. was a very pertinent man, thoughtful and wise. Loquacious in those early days recalling his life and friends, he was also one who favoured silence. I loved the stories. He called me 'a funny girl', 'a good girl', even as I hoped for more, and added, 'you may be many things but you are never uninteresting'. I had never had a sustained love affair with an Australian man, my tastes and geography offering British and American lovers more given to endearments and tender words. It seemed that the male of the species of my own country was less apt in such ways; but action was sweet.

It was lovely to have a warm human in my bed, both of us in need of love and joyously finding it, his face on the pillow, grave at morning. He too was happy. 'So there will be no barriers between us', he said. After the hurt and grief of my shattered marriage, I marvelled at my good fortune. There was, too, a patent change in M. As his friends were wont to tell me, he lost his haggard look. He became a great soaker-up of compliments, and I gladly offered them. We walked among the browsing kangaroos at twilight. 'I'm glad you've come into my life in my old age', he remarks shyly as we stroll, and when I say how extraordinary it is to find him in mine, he adds, pertinently, 'But it's your own fault!'

And so our lives took on a newly measured air. We were both workaholics and with my intermeshing enterprises and interests, I was not demanding of shared time. I had, in fact, taken note of a message M. had received on a card from a close friend at Christmas wishing him happiness with 'his work, his family and Ann'. If the ordering caused me mild demur, I grasped the point. M. was deeply absorbed in his studies in which the past informed the present and knowledge of the present informed and clarified the past, and he had quickly advised me, 'If you are going to knock around with me, you must read and learn about these subjects' (no word here about a reciprocal reading into the history of science!).

He was also clearly devoted to his geographically absent adult children and frequently in touch with them.

We were soon known among friends as an 'item', a word that metamorphosed our more ambiguous state. For I was still married to a husband I was never permitted to see. When, by devious routes at night, I managed to call upon Joe in his small retirement cell, M. was my warm and supportive friend. My tenderness for him grew, as did his for me. I would often say then, 'I love you', and he with a small smile, in character, would reply 'I quite like you'. I knew his teasing well. But, as women are ever eager to learn why someone has fallen in love with them, M.'s reply to that question – 'for the way you have lived your life' – surprised and delighted me. And so I mapped our love affair. 'To be aghast and muddled and fascinated', Rosemary Dinnage had written of such occasions in the *New York Review of Books*, 'is at least a good start'.

Yet these were duplicitous times. 'Trustworthiness'? I kept all news of M. from Joe. And when through 1998 his health deteriorated and the embargo on me lifted briefly I spent hours with him in hospital, it was not difficult for me to offer true endearments and my sense of a long and close companionship and love for him in his stoicism and pain. Can one love two people at the same time? I found it so. It was a curious blend. I was struck by the terrible sadness of my dear Joe's plight: in his most extreme illness his children did not come, and my days were threaded with anxiety. Yet I was in love with M. and he with me.

When Joe died in May 1998, in dignity and quietness, my new life changed. There were different and enlarging elements for M. and me. Our circles of friendships grew. M. appeared a man for friendships – former students, colleagues, diplomats and journalists with whom he shared an expertise, old friends known at school and university, a close web of those with whom he'd served in war. Friends were even rustled out as we jaunted about the countryside. I came to enjoy the warm friendship of his congenial brother and sister-in-law; but, best of all, I would find among his younger friends several who tied me into close affection. Since by nature I was not maternal and had no children, they grew to be vital new families to me.

Now we could spend weeks, sometimes months, together in M.'s house on the Mornington Peninsula, a house of glass with spanning views set amid shrubs and trees. Being driven by work, we had our separate stations with whatever book or article was in the making. But we would interrupt those studious hours with long walks along the rocky beach – a grey-white beach strewn with driftwood, very different from the warm creamy beach sands of Sydney of my younger days. His beach was positioned on Western Port Bay looking out at that 'facing island' of which the historian Jan Bassett had written so evocatively in her book of that name. Walking there alone, at times I would think warmly of this woman historian whom I had never met and the stories she told: tales of her grandmother's life on Phillip Island; of the island's history; and of Jan's own approaching death from cancer at forty-six, foretold and anticipated as she wrote. I found and read her well-researched and sensitive books on women in war. She was clearly much loved by her friends and colleagues, and I wished that I had known her in our historically related, if contrasting, lives.

I had always thought of myself as something of an expert on beaches. I was born in February under the sign of Pisces – two fish swimming in opposite directions – and beaches have given me intense delight. Brought up with childhood holidays at Collaroy Beach in Sydney, I had sunned on them through girlhood;

wandered on Queensland and Pacific Island beaches snorkelled with Joe among brilliant coral reefs; and had been carried under Lord Beaverbrook's affluent care to the jewelled beaches of the Bahamas where their spectacular hues found expression in the evocatively named 'Emerald Beach'. Now I came to love the familiar grey quietness of Victoria's sanded shore.

It begs a question that someone so long an inhabitant of New South Wales and the ACT could know so little of a neighbouring State. Why on this continent are we so geographically insular? With M. a product of Victoria by birth and education, we picked our frequent routes through its blond countryside, loitering beside the Murray River, exploring the flat channel-intersected landscape south of Echuca where he had spent his rural childhood. One of his former graduates and his potter wife lured us to Queensland where we fell in love with Peregian Beach and its stretching span of camel-coloured sand. We soon began an annual trek from Canberra's winter to spend long sunny weeks there, in a neat apartment that looked out on a brilliant sea. We worked, of course, but were linked to the old-fashioned village, the hummingbirds in the bright bougainvillea, and the beach walks at sunset along the colouring shore.

By temperament, we were very different. M. prized the adage, 'silence is golden' while I, a communicator, liked to chat. 'I like talking to you', he once remarked, 'Why not try listening?' It was then that he considered that 'Ssh' would be an appropriate epitaph on my tombstone. He was to all eyes an in-turned man; I the reverse. Yet we shared wide interests and talked with each other about our work. Moreover, a new experience for me, he was my contemporary. As an old friend put it, 'We sat at Joe's feet; M. is an equal'.

And so in this mood of extending scenes of happiness, the old century with its store of privilege and opportunity and grief passed into the new. It would hold a nemesis for me. At the turn of 2000, a chance visit to the local hospital while I was staying on the Victorian peninsula found me diagnosed with cancer of my left kidney, so advanced that it would have to be removed. What gratitude I feel to that anonymous cluster of young doctors drawn from India, China and the Mediterranean at Frankston Hospital, so intent and thorough in their scrutiny, so wise in moving from my temporary and unrelated ailment to an ultrasound that divulged this life-threatening thing. I marvel at my good fortune. Back in Canberra my aloof British kidney surgeon counselled that, while I waited for several weeks to abandon a blood-thinning aspirin tablet I was taking, I should 'get myself fit'. Walking hard and long each day around the suburbs, I did. I felt in high good health and calm. While friends looked stricken at my news, 'the Big C' did not disturb me. For me it was, come what may, simply just an operation. And so it proved. I woke surely only a moment after the anaesthetist crouching behind me had stuck a long needle into my spine to find M. standing with red roses as I lay bedecked with tubes. 'Brave girl', he said: those lovely words. My surgeon, aloof no longer, had told me in Intensive Care that there had been no spread of cancer, and when, later, I queried him about outcomes, he replied, 'You will probably be lucky: we never really know in this line of country'. And so I was.

Convalescence is a time of pleasure, a release from duties and deadlines, coloured by love and peace. My newly met carer, Wilma Robb, appeared smiling and companionable. Her goodnight words, 'I love you' always comforted me. My faithful M. came daily, sometimes in silence, shedding undemonstrative love.

My sister Mimi flew in from Sydney. I had been fortunate on every front. I was due to complete my book *Platypus* and, after my nine days in hospital, my publisher had rung to say how much they liked it. There was a final chapter to go. Yet eager as I was to finish it, I found myself incapable of resuming work. At last I wept. It was the moment to refocus, to consider one's survival and one's days.

M. and I would pick up our varied life. Friends came and went. Some visited from Asia and, staying often at his seaside house, we gathered a new and congenial company. Recovered from my operation, we flew with our friends Romaine and Tony to Western Australia's beauteous Ningaloo Reef. The reef edges the dramatic ochre-red country of the west, with subtle green-and-lavender cabbage corals that stretch away – dramatically different from the flamboyant swaying corals of the Great Barrier Reef. Floating far out at sea with my friends along a lavender coral highway, I thought distractedly for a moment, 'Whatever am I doing here with only one kidney?' But what happiness! 'We will', says M. (a shore man in this exercise), 'go into great old age together'.

CHAPTER 6

AMONG THE HISTORIANS

Australia harboured two great historians in the second half of the twentieth century, Sir Keith Hancock and Manning Clark. Others may offer further names, for this country has been a prolific breeder of historians. But, for me, these two men individually left a singular heritage. Hancock masterminded and founded the *Australian Dictionary of Biography,* hailed as a jewel in the crown of the ANU with its eighteen volumes of historical scholarship; Clark proved to be the greatest historical generalist of his age.

Hancock, as an expatriate, had already wrapped up some luminous posts in Britain – as a young Professor of History at Birmingham University; then pioneering editor of the *Survey of British Commonwealth Affairs* at Chatham House; editor of the *United Kingdom Civil Series* (part of Britain's official World War II history); a Fellow of All Souls, Oxford; and as the foremost Commonwealth historian in an advisory constitutional role in Uganda. He was knighted for his services and, after further experience in South Africa, he returned to his own soil in 1957 as first director of the Australian National University Research School of Social Sciences.

A year or so later I had the good fortune to be recruited by him to assist in building a national dictionary of biography to tell the story of the Australian people. I had already met this small quixotic man in England nine years earlier when, after careful scrutiny, he steered me to a post working with his successor, Nicholas Mansergh, on the Commonwealth Surveys at Chatham House, and, unwittingly, a few years later into Lord Beaverbrook's historical camp. Now, after my high-flying years with the powerful media Lord, he had drawn me back to Australia to his side.

I have written in my earlier memoir of the turbulent times Hancock and I shared building the dictionary structure, notably with the fiery Sydney historian from outside the ivory towers Malcolm Ellis. To write about this time, I had drawn largely on my own memory and my stock of personal correspondence with Hancock while he had been absent at All Souls, Oxford for nine months following the death of his wife, Theadon. But late in 2010, as plans shaped for a history of the *Australian Dictionary of Biography*, I was invited to write the opening essay on the 'Establishment Era', which we would subsequently call 'Sir Keith Hancock: Laying the Foundations, 1959-1961', and enjoyed the hitherto unavailable chance of exploring the now professionally organised *Dictionary* archives at the ANU which, stretching back to 1959, yielded up complex and revealing stories.

The human and administrative plans for getting this major project off the ground proved a constructive part of my historian's career. It had brought me back to the field of Australian history – whose historiography was in its infancy – at a time when the growing State university departments of history were strapped for funds and somewhat envious of the privileged research role and rich government funding of the ANU. While there was apparent interest among the senior Australian historians for the dictionary idea, there was also uneasiness about a national project centred at the Australian National University. I was well aware in those early founding days that Hancock's broad experience placed him high above the other members of the small historical fraternity. Ken Inglis tagged him 'the Archbishop of Australian historians', and it was undoubtedly Hancock's expatriate reputation, his association with Britain's *Dictionary of National Biography*, and his long absence from the Australian scene that enabled him to mastermind the project, build the bridges, and draw the historians of the expanding State and regional universities into a collaborative team.

It was pleasing to me that the archival records confirmed this view. As Hancock himself put it at the time in his reflective prose, 'We went ahead with determination but also with patience. The responsibility for planning had been put upon us. Consultation and discussion were fundamental. At every stage, we submitted our plans to our colleagues in the Australian Universities'. As plans for an editorial board at the ANU took shape, the problem of State participation was happily diffused by Gordon Greenwood, Professor of History at the University of Queensland, who, while pressing the point that the younger staff members of his department had their own careers to make rather than attend to a new national venture, coined the telling words: 'We will do nothing *for* the ANU, but *with* the ANU there are no limits to what we will undertake'. Greenwood's intervention ensured the formation of the National Committee as the *Dictionary* policy-making body and, as Hancock publicly acknowledged, 'We owe him a great debt'.

Nonetheless, it was Hancock, with his dynamism and energy and abiding sense of growth and span, who became the *Dictionary*'s guiding force. As 'the skeleton staff', I was proud to work in tandem with him in the founding days of such a work. The *Dictionary* has now been through six successive general editors, an overarching editorial board, a key national committee, a clamour of State and regional working parties, and the voluntary contribution of an immense army of unpaid writers and assistants. It has been judged by reviewers, as the individual volumes rolled off the production line, as 'an eye-opening source of new biographical knowledge'; 'an enthralling story of the history of Australia told through its people'; 'a unique pathway to social history'; 'a national record'; 'a browser's paradise'; and 'the bedside book of bedside books'. Digitised in 2006 and pushing out new biographical directions, the *ADB* stands now as a unique testimony to historical knowledge and research.

Hancock also worked as a gentle-yet-penetrating influence on the postgraduate students in his department of history, and as an advocate for interdisciplinary themes. His own research centred on a two-volume biography of the prominent, if paradoxical, South African leader Jan Smuts, although Australia's environment would capture him in the end in his path-breaking book *Discovering Monaro*. Along the way, in 1969, Hancock at seventy-one gave rise to the Australian Academy of the Humanities and became its first president, arguing with some amusement that 'unless we take prompt action, senility will overtake us!' Prime Minister Menzies ensured him a second knighthood in 1965 – 'twice a knight at my age' he would quip gaily – while Australia's senior historian Stuart Macintyre contends that 'had there been a Nobel Prize for History, Sir Keith Hancock would have won it'.

In his recent biography *A Three Cornered Life. The historian W. K. Hancock*, historian and writer Jim Davidson has offered a spacious overview of this eminent-yet-somewhat-overlooked man. For me, he was both a vital mentor and an influential friend. I owe him long and affectionate gratitude.

It was during those lively *Dictionary* days that I came to form another lasting friendship, with Manning Clark. Those two greats, Hancock and Clark, enjoyed the admiring-yet-mixed relationship of very different men. As Professor and foundation head of the Department of History at Canberra's University College from 1950, Manning Clark became the first historian to teach a full length university course in Australian history. It was a course which, for the students, shifted the old perception that Australian history 'was dry, peripheral and second rate, not worthy of bright young minds' and empowered them to become pioneers. With the rival establishment of the Australian National University, Clark strongly objected to the division that divorced teaching from research, and emphasised the distinction between the teaching College and the research-centred ANU. Hancock's arrival from Britain in 1957 hence stirred a mild frostiness, but one that was swiftly dispelled when Hancock introduced joint postgraduate supervision between the two institutions. Manning Clark was also drawn into *Dictionary* structures to become a member of the editorial board and an editor of one of its first volumes.

Separated at times by distance, Clark and Hancock shared their historian's zeal. Among the Manning Clark Papers in the National Library, I was intrigued to find a letter Hancock had dashed off to Clark in 1966 when on leave at All Souls, Oxford and wrestling with the revision of the second volume of the Smuts' biography. 'Being a historian', exclaimed this prolific historian, 'is hell: but how could we live without the hell? My own hell now is both grisly and exhilarating, 10 weeks of intense work on revision (29 chapters in draft). This will be, I promise myself, the last time in my life that I shall barbarise myself by excessive concentration on one large task'. Paradoxically, Hancock, whose own work was anchored in the document and who had set about establishing the Smuts Archive in South Africa, destroyed many of his own personal and professional letters and no response from Clark survives.

In contrast, Clark was a historian who not only conducted a vast correspondence but carefully preserved it for posterity, placing it in the National Library of Australia, together with a fifty-year-long highly personal diary as a source for researchers. His own six-volume *A History of Australia* (the 'A' is important), published between 1962 and 1987, had given Australians a lasting gift: a vivid, sweeping track through, and a particular vision of, their own history and its characters great and small. It also offered a keen perception of the self-destroying elements of the human condition that, along with triumph and achievement, made up the history of a nation. It was an intellectual reach that embraced and enlightened the Australian community, but not his fellow historians who tended to drop it from their course reading lists. The volumes, however, in their huge editions, continue to be widely read. Staying in a rainforest resort for Australian and international tourists above Queensland's Cape Tribulation, I would find Manning's well-thumbed volumes on the shelves revealing in that distant outpost the remarkable impact and reach of his work.

In both his history and friendship, Manning Clark was a deeply compassionate man, alert to the ordinariness and extraordinariness of humans. Yet the 'mockers and destroyers' whom he discerned in the country's history also figured in his own contemporary scene and, as he was wont to say, his voice falling, 'There are some faces I wish I had never seen'. I admired him as a writer and loved him as a buoyant friend. 'Mrs M', he would call me as my name flickered from Mozley to Moyal, 'where are we all going; the plants of civilisation are fragile!' My own fields of scientific and technological history in Australia, or women in science – women for the most part anywhere – did not enter his historical frame. I recall consulting Volume 1 to see what he had to say about the scientifically minded Governor Brisbane who brought two trained astronomers to New South Wales in 1821 at his own expense, established the Parramatta Observatory and planted the physical sciences in Australia. But I found only that Brisbane greatly loved his wife! Nonetheless I sent my books to him as they appeared. His friendship ran like a rare thread through my days.

Manning Clark died in May 1991, not peacefully, rather fighting off death and his avowed quest for the time when 'all questions would be answered'. The wide affection that this historian and cultural prophet generated among people of all kinds was manifest among the varied hundreds who gathered at his funeral service at St Christopher's Catholic Cathedral in Canberra, while passers-by stood murmuring quietly among themselves, 'It's Manning Clark's funeral'. In 2000, however, the release of his personal diaries through access provisions with the National Library brought a new and confounding figure to view. Scribbled at night over half a century and yielding up their secrets of self-loathing and doubt, they tore at the chords of love in marriage, an ongoing litany of distrust, betrayal and disappointment. Here was a side of Manning Clark which close friends, myself included, neither recognised nor knew.

How illuminating it has been, then, when two very different scholars, the literary Brian Matthews and the historian Mark McKenna, worked through the diaries and delivered their penetrating views. For Matthews in *Manning Clark. A Life*, creativity lay at the heart of his brilliant-but-tortured subject – a man of masks and presentations with his trademark hat and belt, his rich prose, and his compassion and imagination, yet a man whose mind was tuned to the dark themes of Chekov, Dostoevsky, Tolstoy, and Dickens rather to that of other seminal historians. In part I found this a curiously comforting book, a timeless case study (certainly at its most extreme) of everyone who is deeply engaged in writing with its struggles and sacrifices and its compound of expectation, self-delusion, promise and doubt.

By contrast, McKenna's immense biography *An Eye for Eternity. The Life of Manning Clark* (2011), written by a younger historian who never met his subject, opens the historical world of this 'great generalist in a time of increasing specialism' as he sees him, and he confronts Clark's personally tortured world discerningly. Manning's wife, Dymphna, herself faced the contents of these excoriating personal diaries and hoped not to be alive when they were given public release. Just in time. She died from cancer in May 2000, just before their public release. But, as McKenna perceives, 'Dymphna also knew that Clark's performance did not stop with his death. He had a habit of refusing to lie down'. Divining this personal labyrinth, McKenna observes that there was 'no purely private realm in Clark's writing' but 'a brutal determination to confront his feelings'. His candid diaries became his way 'of making sense of his existence; experience giving shape and form through language stopped the truth from running away'.

McKenna would also find that (in contrast to Manning Clark's often criticised loose approach to accurate referencing in his history) he emerged as a scrupulous recorder for his biographer. 'He was a writer', McKenna notes, 'hunting an audience. Whatever he wrote, the promise of an audience always beckoned'. Far from the quiet authorial footprint, the biographer confronted 'an absolute freeway with signposts and a detailed road map!' Through both his published and unpublished materials, this larger-than-life historian of many themes wished to 'transcend his time'. McKenna's absorbing biography allows him to do so. His conclusion, after a seven-year odyssey, is a jubilant testimony to the man. 'To write Clarke's life', McKenna sums up, 'was to wrestle with an irrepressible leviathan. There was rarely a moment when I could not feel him deploying all his wit, pathos and charm in order to direct this story. He refused to be silent, bobbing up incessantly despite my efforts to restrain him, a mercurial spirit who lived to be remembered. Whenever I picture him, there is always a playful glint in his eye'.

Friendship with Manning Clark had brought me – how the skeins spin out – to his close friend and colleague, historian Don Baker, who since 1950 at Canberra University College and then Manning's Department of History at the ANU had been Clark's closest ally. In my early days of writing about science, I had sent Don – whom I knew but slightly – a copy of a paper I'd written on 'Darwin and the Climate of Opinion in Australia' which I thought might interest him, and received back the warm response, 'I could wish I had written it myself'. Such words are a benediction to a young (or indeed any) writer. I learnt then that he was a great encourager of scholars and the vast cavalcade of students he supervised. Renowned as a teacher, Don in his retirement also became a distinguished scholar and researcher. His outstanding books on the nineteenth-century Presbyterian prelate and reformer Dr John Dunmore Lang, and the scientifically knowledgeable surveyor Sir Thomas Mitchell, were enriching to my own fields of research.

Much later we would come together to organise a portrait to honour the life of Dymphna Clark. Retired then but still hard at his own research, this gentle, humorous man (the wild young man I never knew) also offered me his help with my massive typescript of *The Web of Science. The Scientific Correspondence of the Rev. W. B. Clarke* of which I write later. Don's long-time partner, Pat White, reported how he would rise each morning, relishing the day, and immerse himself in the stretching papers of this document that touched many players and arenas of his own research. His recommendation to Melbourne University Press for the publication of my work (copying me his generous letter which I would find years later among my papers) suggested that the work was analogous to Beaglehole's work on Cook and would bring the press much honour. He died in January 2007. It was only then (though I knew him as a free spirit and an active public protester over Vietnam) that I learnt that he had registered as a conscientious objector in World War II, but volunteered to serve as a malarial-control officer in Papua New Guinea where the disease proved a more deadly enemy than the Japanese.

Historians, however, come in many guises: the deeply penetrating who push out known boundaries; the exploratory; the pioneers who foster large new fields and disciplines – the prehistorians, the rural, military, scientific, economic, women's historians and more; and those who leave a clear trace of their presence on the record. Let me introduce you to one who, for me, stands large in this last coterie, Australia's distinguished poet Les Murray. A poet of the bush and lost phenomenon, Murray has the historian's eye and his images and arguments stride memorably across Australia's historical page. It was my history of telecommunications, *Clear Across Australia*, of 1984, that brought me into personal touch with this gifted man. Reared as a bush boy amid the farms and timber country of mid-northern New South Wales, Les' poems cast a deep and loving gaze upon old discarded rural machinery and the one-time technologies of communication which, finally and inevitably, have yielded place to new, fixing them forever in the cultural record.

I had read his poem 'Morse', published in his collection *The People's Otherworld*, and was inspired to reuse it in a chapter on the Overland Telegraph Line I was writing for Rosaleen Love's edited collection *If Atoms Could Talk* in the late 1980s. I wrote to alert Les, and we continued the correspondence, exchanging books, and I became the recipient of Les' recollections about technologies that had infused his historical themes.

'I seem to have mentioned or written about letters, telegrams, radio, TV, newspapers, heliograph effects, carrier waves, satellites, dish antennae, postcards and much more in the same line as well as about the Morse telegraph', he wrote. 'I am fascinated with machinery and probably write about it more than most poets'. A few months later, having read *Clear Across Australia*'s account of the Bendigo inventor Henry Sutton, who, in 1887, had designed an apparatus he called 'telephany' by which he hoped to bring the Melbourne Cup to the citizens of Ballarat, Murray composed a poem about this theoretical television precursor which he called 'The Tube' and published it in the *Sydney Morning Herald*. He dedicated it to me and his Glaswegian poet mate Rob Crawford, a fan of Britain's television pioneer John Logie Baird. 'See what you've caused!' he exclaimed. He had caught at once at the inventiveness of 'telephany', the technical restraints of so early a period, and life's unseen reverberations.

Yet it is Murray's culturally fused and technologically interconnected poem 'Morse', with its tale of the first medical operation conducted via the telegraph, famous now in the Northern Territory town of Hall's Creek, that has special resonance and will hold enduring place in Australia's history.

> *Tuckett. Bill Tuckett. Telegraph operator, Hall's Creek*
> *which is way out back of the Outback, but he stuck it,*
> *quite likely liked it, despite heat, glare, dust and the lack*
> *of diversion or doctors. Come disaster you trusted to luck,*
> *ingenuity and pluck. This was back when nice people said pluck,*
> *the sleevelink and green eyeshade epoch.*
>
> *Faced, though, like Bill Tuckett*
> *with a man needing surgery right on the spot, a lot*
> *would have done their dashes. It looked hopeless (dot dot dot)*
> *Lift him up on the table, said Tuckett, running the key hot*
> *till Head Office turned up a doctor who coolly instructed*
> *up a thousand miles of wire, as Tuckett advanced slit by slit*
> *with a safety razor blade, pioneering on into the wet,*
> *copper-wiring the rivers off, in the first operation conducted*
> *along dotted lines, with rum drinkers gripping the patient:*
> *d-d-dash it, take care, Tuck!*
>
> *And the vital spark stayed unshorted.*
> *Yallah! breathed the camelmen. Tuckett, you did it, you did it!*
> *cried the spattered la-de-dah jodpur-wearing Inspector of Stock.*
> *We imagine, some weeks later, a properly laconic*
> *convalescent averring Without you, I'd have kicked the bucket...*

*From Chungking to Burrenjuck, morse keys have mostly gone
   silent
and only old men meet now to chit-chat in their electric
bygone dialect. The last letter many will forget
is dit-dit-dit-dah, V for Victory. The coders' hero had speed,
resource and a touch. So ditditdit daah for Bill Tucket.*

My warm tears fall.

CHAPTER 7

DYMPHNA. 'THE GIRL IN THE DIRNDL DRESS'

How do you describe a woman; how define her? Photographs of Dymphna Clark garbed in her hallmark dress of skirt, jumper and Peter Pan collar (serviceable for all occasions) appeared not infrequently in the Australian press, often with Manning at her side, several given permanent place in the iconic photography of Heide Smith. After Manning's death, this strong faced, articulate, informed woman became her husband's staunch defender against his critics and detractors, an outspoken visual presence. In every sense, Dymphna Clark was all the things she outwardly appeared to be: the vital and engaged editor of her husband's books, the mother of six clever children, a generous and hospitable hostess to the hordes of students, friends and colleagues who flocked to the welcoming Clark door, an imaginative cook and inventive gardener. Above all she had the gift of friendship.

I had the good fortune to join in this ever-widening circle. When, with my historical concerns and interests, I initially visited the Clark home to talk with Manning, Dymphna would draw me firmly to her side – an act at first frustrating, but in hindsight linked to a perception that Manning had enough historically motivated bright young women streaming in his wake. Even as susceptible a man as he has proved to be, she need hardly have bothered. Manning in his letters would always send me his 'non-Dionysian love'. No torture there! And I had much to thank her for. She became my vivid and enduring friend.

Behind this competent and outward-flowing woman, however, there were deep complexities. Born in December 1916 in South Yarra, Melbourne, as Hilda Dymphna Lodewyckx to a Belgian father and a half-Swedish, half-Norwegian mother, she was brought up in Melbourne between two wars by parents, who, while taking out Australian citizenship, remained conceptually and politically European. Dymphna was educated at Mont Albert Central School and at Presbyterian Ladies' College in Melbourne. In 1932 she travelled under her mother's care to study German at a Gymnasium in Munich, and entered the University of Melbourne the following year. There, different and somewhat 'foreign', in her own words, she 'stuck out like a sore thumb' in her dirndl dress and socks, 'the mad girl without a hat'. But it was her very 'European-ness' and 'difference' that provoked fellow student Manning Clark to engineer an introduction to her in 1936. As Mark McKenna rightly divined, 'The man drawn to the grand themes of European history fell in love with the European woman who at twenty was fluent in Dutch, German, Italian, French, Swedish, Norwegian and Danish'. By 1938 they were engaged and on their way together overseas, Manning to study on a scholarship at Oxford and Dymphna to study for a PhD in German languages on a Humboldt scholarship at Bonn University.

Dymphna enjoyed Germany but her presence in Bonn on 10 November 1938 during the savage Nazi assault upon the Jews at 'Kristallnacht' – which she described graphically in a letter to Manning at Oxford – led to her leaving Germany at Manning's insistence and to their swift marriage in England in January 1939, her scholarship set aside. Not surprisingly, Manning found his new wife (as he wrote her mother) unhappy the day following their marriage, uncertain what a life without her scholarship would mean. It meant struggle. In an Oral History interview given at the National Library of Australia in 1990, Dymphna recalled their early difficulties where, impecunious with the loss of her scholarship, she was unable to get a job of any kind in immediate pre-war England, except for a short time teaching French at Blundell's School in Devon where Manning was briefly employed, a problem that continued when war broke out. But her course was set. She helped Manning in libraries, attended a few lectures, kept house, and in due time Sebastian, their first child was born. Yet, while the prospect of her personal intellectual future had passed, she saw Manning, as 'far more gifted than anyone else I knew of my own age'. But there was a rider: 'I never expected', she added, 'that he would achieve the celebrity he had achieved. I always envisaged a quieter, more obscure existence where the excitements would be internal and not external'.

The Dymphna I met in 1959 saw herself with characteristic humour as 'a comma and full stops'. However, over the years as children multiplied she struggled for a long time to locate her own being and single-mindedness. As unpaid research assistant to her husband, editing, typing, translating and researching in archives and newspapers, she was, self-acknowledged, 'a backstop' there. 'Not always a willing backstop', she admitted. But when Manning moved to his Professorship at the ANU in 1950, Dymphna seized any available time to plunge back towards scholarship and deploy her extensive linguistic skills translating works in German in the Departments of Linguistics and Pacific History at the ANU, lecturing in German at the Faculties of the ANU, and teaching German to Australian diplomatic cadets. 'Translation', she admitted in her National Library oral interview, was 'a refuge, a great alibi and an outlet. I've translated before breakfast or after midnight; in trains and boats. You are in a little billabong of your own and you don't have to worry about power play because intellectual life can be a jungle'.

Dymphna's sustained commitment to Manning's historical work was a translation of a kind in itself. 'In the early years', she recorded, 'I was the only thing he had in the way of an assistant'. Until his Canberra appointment she was his typist and research assistant, a role she never quite let go. 'I've certainly spent a great deal of time typing, editing, and translating occasionally for him, and discussing things. I have a feeling from a few things he's said recently, that my role has grown with the years but I wouldn't like to say more than that'. Her modesty, in fact, concealed a central truth. As she put it, 'I've always felt very conscious of the fact that I mustn't interfere too much. Very often my version of what had been under discussion would have been very different from his. But I always felt it was not my place to change it'.

Dymphna's words, communicated only after his death, uncover something of the nature of her input into Manning's work. It was only after he started 'to make his mark with what he was doing', she said in interview, that she drew back. It seemed to her then 'that if everybody – no not everybody – but if so many people can find so much in what he has to say and the way he says it, who am I to want to change it?'. Manning's own verdict on her contribution, however, was sure. 'She saved me from myself', he said.

Throughout all her multifarious tasks there was never any sign that Dymphna regretted the loss of a promised scholar's life. Indeed, as she made plain in her second oral interview at the National

Library with her daughter-in-law Elizabeth Cham, she had 'a very old-fashioned attitude' to the role of a wife. 'If a husband has something important to do and say', she declared, 'then it's part of the wife's role to help that along…I am no George Eliot, and no George Sand, nor was I an Emily Dickinson, so I don't think that anything of world moment was sacrificed because I took that role'. A decade older than I, she did not engage with gender themes. Rather her years were full of interest, action and involvement. Environmentally focussed, she managed to plant more than a thousand trees at the family's seaside retreat at Wapengo on the south coast of New South Wales and to cultivate a highly productive garden at the house Robin Boyd designed for them in Forrest, Canberra. A practical visionary she became an active member, along with Judith Wright and Nugget Coombs, of The Aboriginal Treaty Committee in the early 1980s, sponsored wide Aboriginal interests, and involved herself in many community acts of care. Always she remained the most modest and generous of women. When I sent her a copy of *Breakfast with Beaverbrook* in 1995, she replied, 'With all your tremendous output and input and travels, and vicissitudes, and relationships, and glamorous ambience for so many years, I wonder that you find time to chat over a pie with yours truly. You have invested a slice of the twentieth century with the variegated hues of a rainbow, and yet there is a solid sediment that makes your book a work of history as well'. Her words were a rich gift to me.

I also had the advantage during the 1990s of using Dymphna's skills as a sophisticated and original colleague for my edited volumes *The Web of Science* when she translated from the French the long professional correspondence between my nineteenth-century geologist, the Rev. W. B. Clarke, and his Belgian palaeontological associate, Professor Laurent-Guillaume de Koninck of Liège University, on the classification of Clarke's important collections of Australian Carboniferous and Palaeozoic rocks. With a rich roar of laughter, Dymphna always referred to these as 'The French Letters of the Rev. Clarke'! It constituted a vital component of my book. I thought of her always as 'Voltaire's true intellectual' – the true independent scholar.

Her own time for creative scholarship came after Manning's death. Then Dymphna worked on the complex editing and translation of a large recently discovered manuscript written in Gothic script (which fortuitously her father had taught her when she was eight) of the travel diaries of the Austrian aristocrat and soldier, diplomat and botanist Baron Charles von Hugel who, from 1833 to 1834, spent eight months in Australia travelling and recording his views of the colonies and of their unique flora. Published by Melbourne University Press as *New Holland Journal* in 1994, von Hugel's work was judged a forgotten masterpiece that opened a new perspective on colonial Australia. Most significantly, it confirmed Dymphna Clark's place as an outstanding linguist and scholar.

In her last decade, this strong-minded and steadfast woman embraced a further role editing, introducing, and bringing to print a number of Manning Clark's unpublished works. They included *A Historian's Apprentice*, drawn from his unfinished chapters on the writing of his six-volume history; *Speaking Out of Turn*, a collection of Lectures and Talks given by Manning (compiled with the help of Sebastian Clark); and *The Ideal of Alexis de Tocqueville*, Clarke's MA thesis which Dymphna introduced with a lively account of its origin in Oxford in 1938 and their experiences in the scholarly underpinning and building of this work. Published shortly after her death in May 2000, it was dedicated to her memory. Those years immediately after Manning's death were also the period when she fought against two major assaults on her husband's name, the first from Brisbane's *Courier Mail* with their false-yet-persistent allegation that Manning Clark had been awarded the Order of Lenin medal; and, most painfully, the verbal assault from their once-close friend and Manning's publisher Peter Ryan at Melbourne University Press, on the quality of Clark's historical writing.

'She's like a galleon in full flight', observed M. when we visited her early in 2000. It was while I was recovering from my kidney operation and, my mind free to roam, I'd decided that we must have a portrait of this wise and beautiful woman to hang, together with Arthur Boyd's famous portrait of Manning, at Manning Clark House. We found her typing away in her small kitchen and ready to assent. But she was already alert to her own predicament and the cancer that would end her life that May. The portrait hence became a posthumous one, painted from photographs and memory by artist Pamela Houstein who chose to depict her subject in younger mode without the wonderful lines that marked Dymphna's face. Contributed by funding from friends across Australia, the painting now holds a central place in the Manning Clark House drawing room.

It was Dymphna's vision that conceived the plan to make Manning Clark House a cultural centre in Canberra. Stirred by the thought that neither she nor Manning could contemplate the demolition and development as a 'superior residence' of their Robin Boyd house and spacious grounds, she took action. Although Manning, as Dymphna's planning statement of 1998 records, 'is no longer at his desk upstairs', the house and garden and the intellectual life that gathered around it should continue modestly in another form to enrich the cultural life of Canberra and the wider community. Until her death, it did, and her bequest part familial, part cultural, successfully created Manning Clark House as the centre it is today. I was delighted when, cementing my ties, Sebastian Clark invited me to become a patron. The house is no shrine, but rather an accessible cultural centre for continuing, outstretching and timely conversation and exchange, a role it has extended and diversified across the past thirteen years.

Following this creative woman's death, the University of Melbourne, which she had graced in distant times with her eager ranging mind, conferred a posthumous honorary DLitt on Dymphna Clark. Now on her grave, following the loving litany of wife, mother, grandmother, her children have added the singular comment: 'Superb Scholar'. Beside her, Manning Clark's tablet carries the words which Dymphna herself had chosen, 'We shall not look upon his like again'.

I carry an abiding picture of this remarkable pair: my dear friends Dymphna and Manning Clark coming towards me downhill in their car one sunlit evening as I drive up a road in Forrest near their home, linked and laughing together with great happiness. For me, overriding all else, it catches forever the true measure of their days.

Chapter 8

MEETING ALAN MOOREHEAD

It was my clever friends the Clarks who added a further dimension to my life, both personal and professional, by introducing me to the famous expatriate writer, Alan Moorehead. In mid-1965, Moorehead was on one of his rare visits to his homeland (for he had settled with his English family in Tuscany in the postwar period) and was here to complete one of his books located in the southern hemisphere. *The Fatal Impact*, to be published the following year. Since I was also briefly in Canberra from America where Joe and I had moved early that year, to my delight Dymphna and Manning invited me to dine with them and Alan at their Canberra home. And as Dymphna served one of her great *boeuf bourguignon* my meeting with this vital, handsome man struck an enduring spark.

We had both at one time worked for Lord Beaverbrook, Alan as Beaverbrook's most celebrated war correspondent in World War II at *The Daily Express*, and I, in those engrossing years of the mid-1950s, as his personal research assistant when Beaverbrook set about becoming a historian. Together we found much agreement and some differences. Alan judged Lord Beaverbrook an imperious master, politically little akin to his liking, and had cut his connections with him in the immediate postwar years. I, alternately, had found this charismatic figure an enthralling employer and rewarding friend. That intimate dinner á *quatre* was a memorable experience full of ranging conversation and shared opinions and, when at the evening's end I drove Alan to his hotel, he kissed me warmly and suggested I go with him to bed. But, happily married and my husband away in Chicago, I declined. It was, I admit, the only such offer I slightly regretted refusing! But when some thirty years later I plunged into the Moorehead Papers at the National Library, I soon found that the handsome Alan, with his legendary charm, was renowned in private circles for his one-night stands and knowledge proved a great elixir!

I did not meet Alan Moorehead again. He died in 1983. But in the late 1980s, we came together, in posthumous form, when Barbara Beckett of the Sydney publishing firm Mead & Beckett (with whom Macmillan had published my *'A Bright & Savage Land'*) invited me to contribute captions and boxed information, drawn from recent research, for their handsomely illustrated new editions of Moorehead's *Gallipoli* and *The Fatal Impact*. This work, full of old and new insights, confirmed my opinion that Alan Moorehead was one of the most gifted historical writers of his time.

He had first sprung to world attention as a war correspondent of Britain's North African campaigns where his evocative descriptions of men fighting in the limitless desert, and his nose for grand strategy placed him far ahead of other reporters. His reportage stirred the commendation of generals and his editor at the *Daily Express*, and culminated in his best-selling *African Trilogy*. But it was his prize-winning *Gallipoli* that had put him squarely on the world's literary map. His overarching account of that fateful venture – with its participants gathered from Britain, France, Australia, New Zealand, India, and Africa; its record strung with tales of high policy, strategy, land and sea battles, disjunct leadership, and the commitment and sacrifice of brave men braced for heroic fight – became a major historical classic.

Alan Moorehead's passage to this particular work had been circular and contorted. As a schoolboy he had hated the very mention of Anzac: the memorials in country towns, the medals hanging in his school hall, the old men recalling past days, and the drunken celebrations on Anzac Day. So when, as an eager young journalist, he set out from Melbourne in 1936 to Britain and Europe's beckoning worlds, he swore he would never think of exposing himself to the idea of Anzac and Gallipoli again. When, however, an English friend visiting in Tuscany presented him one evening with his Gallipoli diary to read, Moorehead was captivated. He immediately plunged into the official records, existing memoirs and private papers of Australian and British soldiers who had fought on the Peninsula, and visited the wild, precipitous hills of the Dardanelles. Gathering up his materials, he settled with his family on the Greek island of Spetses, near Gallipoli, to write. It was his moment of truth. 'There could', he wrote, 'be no other story like it … It was the military event of the century'. And steeped himself in battlefield conflict, he was the best man to write it.

It was in 2002 that I came to Moorehead once more. The National Library of Australia had invited me to write a small book, on a subject of my choosing, to launch their new series 'An Australian Life'. I at once chose Moorehead. His story would tempt any biographer, for he represented a distinctive phenomenon in the history of Australian writing. From the 1950s through the '70s, when Australian writers were little known outside their own country – Patrick White's books, to his chagrin, were printed in miniscule editions – Moorehead was producing a flood of bestsellers which ran (in their editions of multiple thousands) from *Eclipse, Montgomery The Villa Diana, The Traitors, Gallipoli, No Room in the Ark, The White Nile, The Blue Nile* to *Cooper's Creek, The Fatal Impact* and *Darwin and the Beagle*. Yet despite many readers' vivid recollections of his individual works, Alan Moorehead had disappeared largely from view in Australia. It was time for his rediscovery. Moreover, the National Library held the substantial Moorehead Papers which, resisting lucrative offers from academic libraries in the United States, Alan and his wife Lucy had personally brought to Australia in 1971 and presented them to the Library. They stretched over forty substantial boxes.

What bliss it was then to sit in the quiet manuscript room of the National Library poring over Moorehead's private writings, his lifetime of correspondence, his *New Yorker* essays, the drafts of his books, the voluminous collections of his press cuttings, and the abundant reviews of his work. Among his papers I found a note which surprised me: it had been scribbled by Tom Pocock, his British biographer (whose 1990 book, *Alan Moorehead*, centred largely on Moorehead's wartime life), during the swift week he had spent in Canberra among the Moorehead Papers. The note recorded a conversation he'd had with Manning Clark. Recalling our spirited dinner of 1965, Manning in his romantic way had concluded that I had become Moorehead's 'confidante'. Not so. Or perhaps Manning was well ahead in his timing. For it was only in this new century that I became, unanticipated, Alan's true biographical confidant, locked in intimate contact with this complex man and tuned to his life of singular purpose, restlessness and accomplishment.

Alan Moorehead was one of that cultural push of young Melbourne reporters in the mid-1930s (two decades before the famous cluster of other Australian expatriates Barry Humphries, Germaine Greer and Clive James) who fled to Europe to escape the conservatism and ennui of Australia's provincial cities and, through luck, talent and lively enterprise, ended up as war threatened in key newspaper positions. Joining Beaverbrook's *Daily Express*, Moorehead rapidly became that paper's foreign correspondent in the Mediterranean, stationed in Cairo and, as his brilliant reports flowed in, won the ringing title of 'The Prince of War Correspondents'. Later, in the European campaign, the confident (some said 'cocky') young Moorehead developed a close relationship with Montgomery; was with him at the signing of peace with Germany at Luneburg Heath; and wrote the first postwar biography of the Field Marshal. He was also with the first Allied troops to reach Belsen concentration camp. And there, as other journalists railed against the horrors, Moorehead's reaction was penetrating and mature. 'Why? Why? Why?', he wrote. 'Why has it happened? This is timeless and the whole world and all mankind is involved in it. How did we let it happen?'

And so I wished to know what had shaped this creative young Antipodean and made him one of the most perceptive historians of his time. It soon became apparent that Alan Moorehead's life was keyed to journeying. Even as a boy he had come to believe that he 'had to make things happen'; it was a creed that vivified and shaped his days. Conditioned by long and exciting wars, his wartime books, *African Trilogy* and *Eclipse*, had carried the very breath of vivid life and death. But in those postwar years in Tuscany, frustrated by the honeyed life, his thoughts returned to Africa, a country forever embedded in his mind from his wartime forays. Africa became his creative fulcrum. There his famous book *The White Nile* centred on those romantic nineteenth-century explorers Burton, Speke, Livingstone, Stanley, and Samuel and Florence Baker: 'the old ghosts' who sought to untangle the enduring puzzle of the source of the Nile. And there in *The Blue Nile* he stepped back in time to examine the audacious eighteenth-century journey of Britain's James Bruce and Napoleon's expeditionary drive into Egypt that opened up the sleeping continent and made contact with a company of African rulers – cruel, murderous and ambitious – whom his writing enshrines. In his compelling prose, Moorehead engages the reader in a series of extraordinary reconnaissances, reading the explorers' journals, following arduously in their footsteps – the black nights and the brilliant searing days tangible – and evoking a period and a people that coloured the life of Africa across almost two centuries. At the story's end he himself is there at the Blue Nile joining past and present with his lingering prose.

> *'Lake Tana and the source of the Blue Nile can be visited without difficulty' (he writes). 'With mules and guides one can follow Bruce's route up to the source of the Little Abbai and with a little persistence...one can reach the Tisisat Falls in a day's steady riding from Bahardar. It is a rewarding journey. Toward evening one sees in the distance the glimmering cloud of spray rising over the fall. The spray that falls like gentle rain, wetting one to the skin, falls forever – two centuries or more ago on Lobo and Bruce, now on oneself, and still upon any traveller who chances to be at that beautiful place at this present moment. Sometimes a log, borne along by the current, teeters*

for a moment at the lip of the vast abyss, and then plunges downward on its long journey to Egypt and the sea'.

Not surprisingly, it was his friendship with that other maverick expatriate Sidney Nolan that brought Alan Moorehead back to his own country and to the journey of Burke and Wills, a subject that held all the themes that engaged him: exploration, travel, landscape, brave men committed to discovery, and the fearful challenge of the unknown. It was his first real encounter with his own country and the sense of antiquity, mystery and curious beauty that Nolan's canvases evoked. Here he tracked the explorers' footsteps through the unrevealing bush and the empty desert to the edge of the Gulf of Carpentaria and back to the 'Dig Tree' at Cooper Creek where, thwarted by their rendezvous party's departure that very morning, Burke, Wills and young King began their desperate trek southwards 'aliens in this hard indifferent country, this gaol of interminable space'.

Moorehead came to form a very personal view of this Australian epic. It was, he believed, quite unlike the story of those deeply motivated men, the giants of exploration in Africa, or men pitted heroically against men as he had seen it on the battlefield. Rather he saw these as ordinary men lifted into extraordinary circumstances. 'This was just death, stark, despairing and meaningless', he wrote. The quarrel was with that 'old indestructible', the Australian bush. Published in 1963, *Cooper's Creek: The Real Story of Burke and Wills* became a landmark book and an international bestseller which, as Manning Clark was quick to note, put Moorehead out in front of a huge swell of interest starting in the history of Australia.

Reading his twenty or more books immersed among his papers, was also an encounter of a special kind. For, despite his urbanity and accomplishments, Moorehead was a consumed and restless figure travelling and writing to return, re-energised, for periods at his Tuscan home. 'I only know how to live like a hermit or a rake', he once confided to his friend Geoffrey Dutton, while Manning Clark, who met him several times during his Australian visit in 1965, saw him as a solitary and lonely man, always 'something of a fugitive, always on the move'. But with *Cooper's Creek*, Moorehead had returned to his roots. His critical, controversial book *The Fatal Impact. An Account of the Invasion of the South Pacific 1767–1840* would anchor him further in the southern hemisphere, where he turned his camera eye on the effects of that great navigator Captain Cook's several voyages in the Pacific and their impact – albeit unwitting – on the culture of the people of Tahiti; the future of the Australian Aborigines; and the wildlife of the sub-Antarctic islands, plundered by whalers and sealers who followed in his wake.

'And so', Moorehead reflected in his *Fragment of Autobiography*, 'a writer's books are the chapters of his life'. But life with all its glamour and achievement was to deal him an unanticipated instalment. Suffering from headaches, in December 1966 he entered London's Westminster Hospital for a check. 'I'll write about it', he told his family gaily. But the dye administered to reveal any vascular abnormality – in those experimental days of the angiogram – precipitated a mayor stroke that affected his communication nerve. Thereafter, this great communicator could neither speak, read, nor write. He was 56. 'I am one of the lucky ones', he had said of his writing life. He died seventeen years later. The small headstone that marks his grave in a Hampstead cemetery reads simply, 'Alan Moorehead. Writer'.

For me it had been an intimate and enlarging journey. I was crossing boundaries; from history through biography into literary studies. It was a writer's life – and the life of a historical writer – that I portrayed in *Alan Moorehead. A Rediscovery* which the National Library of Australia published in 2005. Personal papers, however, have their own trajectories. Moorehead's papers mirrored his many complexities. His thrusting interests, his passionate dedication as a writer, yet his occasional uneasiness and lack of confidence.

But his writer's creed was clear. 'Never write for the market, only yourself; never write anything unless you are agog to express yourself; rewrite everything until the words are absolutely clear and simple; never be satisfied with anything'. Although he came increasingly to admit that he hated the daily, weekly, monthly process and grind of writing, he relished 'the sense of fulfilment a creative man has that he is on the right track and working to the limit of his powers'.

Moorehead's powers proved formidable. Delivering the Seymour Lecture on Biography in Australia in September 2008, the doyen of British biography Richard Holmes began his lectures by exhibiting the cover of what he graciously called 'Ann Moyal's fine biographical monograph' on a large screen and noting the significant contribution Alan Moorehead had made to creating a new sense of Australia's identity. For Holmes, Moorehead's three powerful books *Gallipoli*, *Cooper's Creek* and *The Fatal Impact* had marked 'a significant type of collective biography' which had been 'decisive in changing public attitudes'. Such summation was expert and confirming. The themes of 'warfare and friendship, exploration and personal endurance, colonial exploitation and ethical responsibility' which Moorehead had pursued (said Holmes) had become major Australian themes and had 'alerted the world to a different Australian cultural viewpoint and helped to establish a new postwar Australian identity for Australia'.

From my close encounter, I salute him.

CHAPTER 9

THE WRITERS' HOUSE

My involvement with Alan Moorehead was to open a new window on my own writing world. It led me to a place rich in memories. I drive through the green rural countryside from Canberra; sweeping up the broad highway to the Blue Mountains; through the old towns Glenbrook, Blaxland, Springwood, Wentworth Falls, and Leura – all latched in my mind to childhood on a journey that drew me back to those remembered days when every year my family would travel by train up the mountain route through the tunnels of the Great Dividing Range – hand carved a century before – to spend a winter holiday in Katoomba. There, with faithful regularity, we would stay for two magic weeks at the Commonwealth Bank flats behind the bank on main street, which, as a senior member of its Sydney staff, my father could secure. We invariably chose the winter months, and each morning we would gaze out with excited joy upon the rim of mountain ranges wrapped in deep white fog, mystic and beguiling to children. There, too, we would leave my mother to prepare our fortifying lunch and dinner (as mothers did) while my sister and brother and I accompanied my father, clearly a great walker, on the long march to the Leura Cascades or the Bridal Falls, and on around the cliff walks to Echo Point where we shouted reverberating cooees across the valleys.

My purpose now is different. Seventy years on I'm off to stay at Varuna, the Writers' House at Katoomba on the edge of the mountains in their haze of ineffable blue. In 2002 I had won a three-week fellowship to the House to complete my biography of Moorehead. Varuna, the former home of novelist Eleanor Dark and her medical husband, Dr Eric Dark, had been bestowed by their son Michael Dark in his mother's memory as a Writers' House dedicated to the continuance and growth of Australian literature. Run by the Eleanor Dark Foundation, it has grown and flourished since its foundation in 1991 as a place for the nourishment and refreshment of writers of every kind. 'Talent develops in a quiet place', said Goethe, true to a high degree at Varuna.

Born in that fruitful year of 1901, Eleanor Dark was an outstanding figure in Australian literature. From the 1940s she achieved both reputation and readership for her monumental historical work *The Timeless Land*, the first in a trilogy of volumes she published, along with a cluster of perceptive novels – *Prelude to Christopher, The Return to Coolami, Waterway, The Little Company, Sun Across the Sky, Lantana Lane, Pilgrimage* and *Slow Dawning* – which focussed contemporary social and intellectual issues, and portrayed the experience of women and their desire for agency in Australian society. Widely read, her novels reflected a sense of country and of personal experience rare in Australian authors of her time.

The Timeless Land, published in 1941, addresses the first five years of Australian settlement from 1788 to 1792, and marks the first piece of imaginative historical writing on the arrival of British convicts and settlers on Australian shores seen in part through Aboriginal eyes. For this task, Dark had plunged into the Mitchell Library to research early diaries, letters and official reports of the period and to acquaint herself with a glossary of Aboriginal words. With these she blended history with fiction, mixing the raw material of harsh settlement with tribal songs and phrases which she borrowed from about the country. The book was acclaimed 'a unique and moving novel', a work of 'extraordinary depth and moral perspective', and was adopted in Australia as a school text. Reprinted in many editions, it remains in print today.

Dark's view of the Aborigines was searching and aware. 'The Australian Aboriginal had great virtues', she wrote. 'In a fairly extensive reading I have been able to discover no vices save those which they learned from the white invaders of their land. Some of their customs seem cruel to us. Some of ours, such as flogging, horrified them. The race is nearly gone, and with it will go something which the "civilized" world has scorned too easily, "life, liberty, and the pursuit of happiness" – to us a wistful phrase, describing a faraway goal – which sums up what was, to them, a taken-for-granted condition of their existence'. She was one of the first writers to use the term 'invaders' of the British arrival and, while she claimed only a rudimentary knowledge of Aboriginal beliefs, was the first to penetrate the ambience of those early contact days when British settlers first mingled with the indigenous people.

Her intuitive gaze sensed the lack of substance felt by the emigrant Australians in this gaunt ancient land, seeing them as plagued by 'a curious sense of impermanence and insignificance, of drifting as though they were ghosts or clouds or shreds of smoke between earth and sky'. Manning Clark was one who responded instantly to Dark's sense of place, and to her skill as a novelist whose writing lent dramatic impetus to historical events. He saw her as one of 'life's enlargers' and, in his early lecturing days at Melbourne University, sought her out as guest lecturer for his honours students. Sending her a copy of the first volume of his *A History of Australia*, he wrote, 'If there is any value in the work at all this comes in part from the inspiration in reading *The Timeless Land*'.

Eleanor Dark died in 1985. Now her spacious, yellow-painted house – with the garden of vivid flowers and native plants she cultivated, and the garden studio in which her work was crafted – offers stimulus and tranquillity to new generations of writers. Little is changed: sunshine enfolds the dining room, and wood from the garden's trees fuels its winter fires.

My first visit to Varuna had a certain edge. Feeling much honoured, I was given Eleanor's master bedroom (a grand choice among the cosy smaller suites) with its high double bed, an old fashioned bathroom, and a veranda studio where a large desk and bookshelves, complete with dictionary and thesaurus, await the scholar. Yet, thrilled as I was to be given the master suite, I was anxious about sleeping in a famous writer's room. In England a few years earlier I had had an unnerving experience. Visiting an American historian colleague, I found him on study leave lodged with his family at Virginia and Leonard Woolf's former home, 'Monks House', at Rodmell, Sussex. The house had been purchased by the nearby University of Sussex and leased to distinguished short-term visitors on the provision that it be maintained as nearly as possible to the exact state in which it had been when the Woolfs had lived there. Virginia's sister Vanessa Bell's bright-hued pots decorated the drawing-room shelves, while the winged-back chair so favoured by T. S. Eliot stood in elegant repose. The spacious garden held the sculptured busts of Leonard and Virginia, her grave eyes gazing out towards the river in which, in 1942, she drowned.

I had long been a devotee of Virginia's writing and her spirited defence of independence and careers for women in *A Room of One's Own*. My joy, therefore, was great when offered her bed-sitting-room study in the garden in which to sleep. True to old custom, the large room still had a dangling ceiling light, no bedside lamp and, simply furnished, held only a single bed, a wide writing table pushed up against the wall, and a chair. That night, happily installed, the windows locked against the chill autumn air, I placed my toilet bag on the table and slipped into sleep, dreaming of the stories Woolf had written in this room. Soon after midnight, however, I woke to the violent noise of things being hurled about the room. Too terrified to move to find the light switch at the door, I froze, petrified in bed.

Morning revealed a tempest of activity. My face creams and lipsticks lay flung wildly about the small room. Yet there was no exterior access to the study, no animal within, and my hosts and I greeted the startling sight in wonder and alarm. We could find no explanation for the strange event. But when, returned to Canberra and dining one night at High Table at University House, I sat beside the visiting American writer Leon Edel (distinguished biographer of Henry James and an authority on the Bloomsbury group) and told my story, he looked at me gravely. 'I am certain', he said quietly, 'that was Virginia'.

Clambering, then, into the high bed at Varuna that first night, I put out the light with apprehension and awaited Eleanor's possible approach. All was benign.

> *Here in the kindly warmth, the beating rain outside…* (she had written of her house)
> *You sleep content…*
> *Another evening crying to my memory*
> *Rain in the night outside and firelight in the room*

'Writers make it at Varuna according to their own style', said its long-time creative director, Peter Bishop. Yet for the five scholars residing there each week, a rhythm of living takes shape. Rising early, one prepares a quick breakfast in the friendly, invitingly old-fashioned kitchen from the store of food; the day is free to write and think. No one seeks your company, no ringing telephone peals. In a house of comfort and silence, the mind is free to roam. There is a gift of space and time. The changing weather of the Blue Mountains taps at the veranda window pane – bright sunshine, a sudden deluge, stormy gusts, grey mists and lively hail. Wrapping my face in a scarf, I take an afternoon walk around the cliff face listening to the sound of distant waterfalls and the screech of cockatoos soaring above the valleys. A lordly landscape.

It is not without its mysteries. In 1957 that master of ancient civilisations, the renowned Australian archaeologist and pre-historian Gordon Childe, chose these plunging valleys as his last site. Out from Britain on a lecture tour of Australian universities, he plummeted to his death in the Blue Mountains at Govetts Leap. Enigmatically, he left his hat and spectacles and his compass pointing to distant Pulpit Rock. A note in his hotel room confirmed his plan. It would not, I reflect as I wander, be difficult today to cast off into one of those lush green valleys. But back at Varuna a comforting evening meal awaits, and lively conversation.

Since my introductory stay I have become a frequent visitor and an alumni at Varuna. No doubt the oldest resident, I find myself surrounded by a company of younger women, usually novelists. There is curious alchemy in Eleanor's house. Relaxing over dinner, talking of writing, an intimacy forms as we pool our life experiences and draw encouragement and interest from one another. For each of us – whether young, middle aged, older professional women or perhaps mothers balancing children and writing at home – to write is our mainspring, life in our differing backgrounds untenable without it. We are of a kind and our swift liaison springs from candour and instant warmth. My new friends, I see, are plucking *Breakfast with Beaverbrook* from the library shelf. At week's end we are loath to part.

Recently I received an email from one of these writers, Vivienne Ulman from Melbourne. 'You may not remember me', she began. I did. On this occasion I had just arrived at the House and was entering the front hall with my bags swinging when a small dark woman jumped out at me. 'I've been waiting to meet you', she exclaimed. 'I want to talk to you about Alzheimer's. 'Goodness!' I thought, 'I may the oldest here, but this is carrying things too far!' And so her message ran:

'I think I was rather rude to you when we first met. At that time I was thinking about beginning to write a book that would be part memoir about my experience dealing with my mother's Alzheimer's and my father's great love and care of her, and part family history in particular with my father's relationship with the ALP and the textile and manufacturing industry in Melbourne.

'You were just beginning to look at your diaries and thinking about the second volume of your memoirs. You were tremendously encouraging about the value of my story and I remember after we went out one afternoon for coffee, I ran upstairs and wrote the whole of the first draft of a chapter. I haven't finished the book yet but a short time ago I submitted it to a publisher who accepted it immediately. I think I owe a lot to Varuna. I'm enormously grateful to you. I'm not sure I'd have had the confidence about the material without our conversations. You'll always be associated in my mind with this book, whose working title is "Alzheimer's: A Love Story".'

I treasure her words. She published with success.

On one of my visits, two young people of Aboriginal descent, David King and Elly Chatfield, arrived at the invitation of a resident, a participant in Varuna's program of mentoring and connecting with the local indigenous people. Both visitors belonged to the region's Gundungurra people and both were victims of the 'Stolen Generation'. David, while reared as a concealed suburban child (to hide the colour of his skin), had eventually learnt to penetrate his mother's country and stories and had been elected a Gundungurra elder. With Elly, he was the first Aborigine to visit Varuna. He quickly noted Aboriginal markings on the native trees around the grounds which denoted this as 'a safe place', 'a women's place'. Here were the signs of 'women's business' and a lineage of women's bonding. His evidence came as a gift to us. It endorsed our personal experience as residents of Varuna and illuminated Eleanor Dark's deeply intuitive understanding of the indigenous people and their sense of presence on this land. 'Life is fluid', she had written in *The Timeless Land*, 'nothing is permanent, everything is connected. The individual doesn't exist alone. We are part of an endless story'.

At Echo Point, where once in distant days we had called out our 'cooees' above the protective railings, there is now a wide layered terrace where elegant sandstone plinths carry the resonant messages of well known writers. 'This kind of view of an immense gulf opening before me and stretching a great distance through the trees was quite novel to me and very wonderful', wrote young Charles Darwin in his diary in January 1826 having ridden out to the Blue Mountains as the *Beagle* lay in Sydney Harbour. The ghosts of history now mesh with the clamouring streams of tourist life. 'The mists', says Elly Chatfield, 'are full of spirits'. For me, once child and now historian, these mists and mountains are also alive with ghosts – the ghosts of explorers who pushed their way through the rugged ranges, the convicts who built the roads that followed, and the early settlers who stamped their names on crests and streams and valleys. There are writing and painterly ghosts, travellers, bushwalkers, and for me, persisting, the memory of my loving parents.

CHAPTER 10

'A LONG CHAIN OF CLEVER PEOPLE'

Memory is the great elixir; without memory, as is widely argued, there is no history. In the personal realm certain individuals entrap it and carry a lasting resonance of a period, a defining time. In her spacious biography of Leonard Woolf, Victoria Glendinning writes evocatively of 'a long chain of clever people' at Cambridge University with whom Woolf spent his student days. There they were – Lytton Strachey, Clive Bell, Maynard Keynes – significant, enduring, influential, spilling into vivid life and remaining with Woolf through his marriage to Virginia and on as he wrote his six autobiographies.

My university days at Sydney, the oldest university in this country, had not produced anything like that striking roll-call. It was wartime in the 1940s, there were only about two thousand university students in the country, and many creative people had gone to war. Most of my friends, with their newly minted Arts degrees, moved into teaching and librarianship – the major outlets for tertiary-educated women – and marrying early, raised clever children, their contribution to society marked. For me, conversely, university education had proved a launch pad to a wider world abroad. It was not until I returned to Australia nearly a decade later and took up residence among the lively community at ANU's University House that Glendinning's phrase lit up a brilliant chain. For it was there that I would meet my distinguished husband J. E. Moyal and a clutch of young staff and scholars on the edge of brilliant careers. They numbered among them the remarkable earth-scientist Ted Ringwood, the witty Austrian-born philosopher Kurt Baier, American anthropologist and authority on the New Guinea's Chimbu Paula Brown and her social-science husband Robert Brown, and the young microbiologist Gwendolyn Woodroofe, who was to carve her name in key work on myxomatosis with Frank Fenner. Sir John Eccles dined nightly at High Table and the brilliant demographer Norma McArthur lent vigour and range.

It was there, too, that I met the artist, illustrator and writer, Nancy Parker. I loved her from the start. She was married to Robert Parker, then Reader in Public Administration at the University and, vivid and original, was making a name for herself in Australian artistic circles after several years of absence across the Tasman. The founding Master of University House, Dale Trendall, was her cultural ally – a fresco of her crayon drawings depicting spare Australian trees set against brilliant yellow mounts hung in the House's upstairs Dining Room. Later, a New Zealander himself, Trendall helped her to a travelling scholarship to extend her art in Italy. Her imaginative images of Roman and allegorical themes, and a small abstract painting of pale-blue leaves, adorn my house where they affirm their distinctive presence after half a century.

Joe and I individually were great acquirers. 'I have always thought of my paintings as children for whom I was glad to find a nice home', I found Nancy writing in her late autobiography

Telling it to Abi, 'When someone bought one it seemed to prove that a child of my imagination was wanted and would be loved'. 'About this time', she noted, 'Ann Mozley, a historian, had come to work with Keith Hancock on the *Australian Dictionary of Biography* and Joe Moyal was Reader in Mathematics at ANU. When they decided to marry we were delighted. It was especially warming to see on their walls, when they moved in together, examples of my paintings and drawings each had bought unknown to each other when single. A rare case of compatibility. In that house, I felt my modest works were especially loved'.

In the prevailing fashion of Canberra academic marriages at the time, Nancy and Robert Parker divorced later in the 1960s, Robert to marry Cecily Burton, John Burton's former wife, and Nancy in time to find great happiness with the illustrious, widowed Geoffrey Sawer, Professor of Law at the ANU. Joe and I would visit them at 'Ecco', their retirement house above the sea at Guerilla Bay which Nancy had designed and built with her three children and where, amid the old trees, the rich green foliage and Geoff's fecund vegetable garden, she stamped her individual artistry. She also wrote short stories, memorable in their perceptive reach. She had an artist's eye and a writer's ear.

In her great old age – when Sawer had died and she, perforce, had moved to a cottage in a retirement village on the South Coast – M. and I became her frequent guests. Listening to our at-times contesting conversation, she presented me with a small, sculptured fabric chicken with the words 'Don't chicken out!' I loved her intrepid character, her capacity to move on, to reflect and absorb. Even when she aged into her nineties and I had to initiate all our telephone contacts, they held vivid and amusing words. We thought she would live to be a hundred. She almost did. Along the way, alas, she passed beyond my reach.

There was an old adage, out of date now in contemporary times, that it was not possible for a woman to have deep friendships with men that fell outside 'relationships' – that allusive if somewhat narrow term. Perhaps other kinds of attachments can grow more readily when, older, one is less encompassed in close partnership. Yet who was the sage who said 'each friend represents a new world in us, and it is only by this meeting that a new world is born'? During the early nineties I met a man who, emerging from a different background, offered me a rare gift of new experience and knowledge.

Alastair Morrison was widely known and much loved in Canberra. The son of the famous Australian journalist George Morrison, ('Chinese Morrison' as he was known) who, for many years was the Peking correspondent of The [London] Times, Alastair was born in Peking in 1915 and reared in Britain. He had a romantic career. After graduating from Cambridge, he took off to Peru and Chile to collect bird specimens, fascinated by 'those beautiful creatures and great travellers', shipping them back to the British Museum and private collectors in England and becoming a great traveller himself. In 1940 he fetched up in Shanghai where his journalist brother, Ian Morrison (long remembered as the British wartime lover killed in the Korean War in Han Suyin's *A Many-Splendoured Thing*), worked as correspondent for *The Times*. From there Alastair moved to Peking, then occupied by the Japanese, and became a cipher officer in the British Embassy Intelligence staff and it was there, in a city that forever marked him, that he met the small, young, smiling German photographer,

Hedda Hammer. After intrepid wartime service in Intelligence in India, Malaya and Chungking, Alastair returned to Peking in 1946, and he and Hedda were married.

'I was a rare bird like Hedda in Peking', he reflected mildly. 'She was a rare bird taking photographs. There was a sort of inevitability about our coming together' (as if it wasn't the most wonderful consequential thing that ever happened to him!). Thereafter he and Hedda spent twenty years in Sarawak, Borneo, where Alastair rose high as an administrator in the British Colonial Service and Hedda's work as a gifted photographer took further distinguished form. They came in time to live in Canberra, where Alastair, with his long background in Intelligence, became a senior member of the Joint Intelligence Bureau of the Australian Department of Defence.

I met him in 1992, a tall gentle figure in his mid-seventies, his rich life's trajectory coalesced into a character of mingled perceptions and concerns. Ornithologist, sinologist, collector of rare Asian artefacts, philanthropist, and the author of two engaging memoirs, *The Road to Peking* and *Fair Land Sarawak*, he was a man whose friendship and recollections opened up large new territories. I did not have the pleasure of knowing Hedda who had died in 1991. But, after her death, Alastair bestowed due prominence on her remarkable old-China photography with exhibitions at the National Library and Sydney's Powerhouse Museum, and the publication of her *A Photographer in Old Peking* – in itself a vital cultural and historical record. One day he took me, rather dauntingly, up a steep hill in the ACT's Namadgi Park to the place where he had scattered Hedda's ashes (for the two of them had been intrepid bushwalkers). Her strong presence in his life remained pervasive: her photographs lined the corridor walls of his large apartment complementing his carefully gathered collections of Asian pots and brasses, and the Afghan and Persian rugs that flashed colour from his floors.

Alastair attended the launch of *Breakfast with Beaverbrook* in 1995 and was the first to bring me back an opinion of the book. Though he had only one eye, he telephoned to tell me that he had read it across two days without a pause and, truly modest, observed, 'I did not know you well before: now I am in awe of you!' My response to this immensely informed and eclectic man was not of awe, but of affection and delight. His capacity for friendship drew in the widest coterie. A congerie of scholars, writers, artists, ornithologists, diplomats, Asianists, collectors, librarians, scientists, journalists, bushwalkers, poets, and environmentalists, grew around him – all the more remarkable, it seemed to me because, in voice and kind (despite his Australian father), he belonged to an English culture. At ninety-three, fragile, deaf and almost completely blind, installed away from his brilliant hangings and adornments in a nursing home, he remained (the visitor's voice speaking close to his ear) the most pertinent and ranging conversationalist I knew. He died after a fall early one morning, a few weeks short of his 94th birthday. Characteristically he had laid down instructions and funds that, after his funeral, all his friends should come together for lunch at his favourite restaurant 'The Rubicon'. He had crossed the Rubicon with a wave.

One's older life is inevitably fractured by friends who have succumbed to debilitating illnesses. Another link in the chain of clever people, the elegant John Hoyle, was a former diplomat of sartorial pride and marked accomplishment who, from remote and often difficult outposts, would send me thoughtful and generous words having read one of my books. We had been students of history together in our University of Sydney days and had dallied companionably over cups of coffee between our respective researches at the Mitchell Library. Even then, with his sharp and witty mind, John Hoyle had a distinctive air. From places as disjoint and distant as Jamaica, Belgrade, Bangladesh, Israel, Sweden and Yugoslavia, he served in complex sites of diplomatic influence while his medically trained wife, Mary Hoyle, a spirited feminist, became official medical adviser to the Commonwealth Department of Foreign Affairs.

In that demanding role she would set off on important missions to diplomatic posts around the world imparting guidance on a kaleidoscope of local diseases and serving as presiding guardian over the health of Australia's diplomatic officers and their families. I remember how, after the Chernobyl explosion, she rang me before departing at a few hours notice to areas down wind from the Soviet's nuclear disaster to gather facts about nuclear fallout. I was working at the time on the politics of the nuclear debate in Australia and trembled to think of myself as a major source on radiation fall-out. Fortunately she had other links. Mary and I, long in friendship, sat together beside John's resting couch in an elite nursing home where his mobility and verbal communication had been stalled by Parkinson's Disease, feeding his silence with reminiscence and talk of present occupations. 'Affection plus intelligence', wrote Miles Franklin, 'is the most delightful mixture of friendship, and friendship the warmest most permanent thing in this existence'. Writing this late in 2012, I learn that John is free at last from his last, most exacting, posting.

I have had good fortune in a diverse career. Colourful figures have stirred my thinking, illuminating, interconnecting, and standing firm in my mental frame. During and since my days as a science-policy scholar, the encyclopaedic politician and intellectual Barry Jones has remained a singular presence in an important field. In my time as Director of the Science Policy Centre at Griffith University in the late 1970s, I was occasionally asked by the Minister of Science in Malcolm Fraser's conservative government, Senator Webster, to set down ideas and outlines for his parliamentary speeches. Greatly to my relief they were never used. For Webster became renowned for his evident want of scientific knowledge and was naughtily taunted by members of the Labor Opposition with questions about the state of some fictitious biological species or other prank. The Opposition Shadow Minister of Science was the lethargic and humorous Dr Dick Klugman whom I had known in my undergraduate days when he was studying medicine at Sydney University. But then came Barry Jones.

In his autobiography, *A Thinking Reed*, Barry has written an adroit, part-dark, part-amusing chapter 'Ministering to Science' which yields an absorbing overview of what he describes simply as 'a hard slog throughout the 1980s to raise consciousness about scientific issues'. The chapter, however, stands as a unique and important personal ministerial survey of science policy in a country which has never taken science and technology as seriously as other industrialised countries are known to do. Barry Jones' period of endeavour in this confronting arena dates from his position as Shadow Minister, appointed first by Bob Hawke and then Bill Hayden from 1980 to 1983, and later in the Hawke Government as Minister for Science, renamed Minister for Science and Technology from 1983 to 1990.

In those early years as Shadow Minister for Science, Barry had become preoccupied with technological change and its likely impact on the workforce, publishing his seminal book *Sleepers Wake! Technological Change and the Future of Work* in 1982. This swept into several swift editions, some twenty-six reprints, and a cluster of languages, but was duly shunned by his parliamentary colleagues, the Australian Press Gallery, the media, the bureaucracy, and business. 'Far too erudite for me, Comrade', said Gough Whitlam. Even before the book's publication, Barry was engaged in formulating ideas for a technological and information society in Australia. From wide reading he was aware of the threat, and promise, that computer technology would bring to a globalised society. In this he found support from Australia's distinguished information economist Professor Don Lamberton who, while widely reputed abroad, was not a prophet in his own country where fellow economists turned a blind eye to the importance of this field. 'Lamberton', writes Jones, 'was the first Australian economist to grasp what was happening and I was the first politician!' It did them no good. They were both 'too far ahead of the pack'.

Despite Jones' attempts with different Cabinets, he failed to establish his carefully crafted National Information Policy. In fact, during his more than twenty years as an MP, as he laments, in this entire critical period, neither the House of Representatives nor the Senate, regardless of party, had a debate about the information revolution or the scope of information policy. His initiatives sank into a black hole.

What baulked this wizard on the political stage? It speaks volumes about that period and the nature of our political institutions that Jones' colleagues were more likely to scatter at his approach along the parliamentary corridors than share any enthusiasm for his far-reaching schemes. The doyen of the Press Gallery Alan

Reid, paraphrasing Goering, articulated the prevailing climate of opinion: 'When I hear the words science and technology I close up my typewriter'. But scientists held Barry Jones in affection and regard. Across his ministerial career he proved a committed advocate for their creative responsibility against a growing administration and political ethos at CSIRO and, while he railed at times against the scientists' failure to develop as lobbyists and public communicators and called them 'wimps', he endeared himself to their community. He now carries the distinction of becoming the only person in Australia to be elected a Fellow of the four elite scholarly academies, the Australian Academy of Science, the Academy of the Technological Sciences and Engineering, the Academy of the Social Sciences in Australia and the Australian Academy of Humanities. What a polymath!

I cherish a deep affection and admiration for him. Across the years he has read my books, pointed out errors, and once enthusiastically married me off to Lord Beaverbrook when reviewing *Breakfast with Beaverbrook*. A warm and receptive friend, he remains always something of a phenomenon. As his intellectual sparring partner and long-time companion Phillip Adams writes of him with truth and fondness: 'Barry is unsparingly honest. Approaching his final years he has yet to learn cynicism. Denied the carapace so often worn in the political world, he retains his sincerity and vulnerability. He cannot help but tell the truth'.

As we all are, I am in Ulysses' famous phrase, 'part of all that I have met'. In the world of work, some may be no more than an interesting transient contact, while others remain vital in shared professional concerns. Robyn Williams has stirred and sparkled at the ABC's 'Science Show' for the greater part of four decades where he has brought insight, understanding and humour to the world of science. I encountered him early in his Australian career when in 1977 he visited my Science Policy Centre at Griffith University and I invited some of the younger scientists to dine with him. There, with due irreverence, he was already nicknaming the 'old farts' as he called the distinguished Fellows of the Academy of Science among whom, with no notable addition of gravitas, he has now been elected. Thereafter, when I became a member the ABC's Science Advisory Committee, I would meet Robyn stretching his glossy scientific wings. For a man who was to become so innovative and important a science broadcaster, Robyn, progeny of a Welsh father and a part-European mother, had the good fortune to attend a North London College where he did the last of that all-embracing British Honours B.Sc degree designed originally by the great science-educator and 'Darwin's Bulldog', T. H. Huxley. It contained taxonomy and anatomy and 'everything you could mention about science, to which were later loosely added genetics, physiology and biochemistry' all of which offered a perfect training for his future career. 'I'd heard of every concept', Robyn recalled in an Oral History interview I did with him at the National Library. 'We were the last ones to take this immense old gargantuan truck of a course. I had no idea what it meant, but I took a curious interest and was very well primed. So I was terribly lucky'. He ended up in Sydney with Peter Pockley, who was founding director of the ABC Science unit, in 1972.

Transforming the old 'talking-head' science programs, Robyn became the science-communicator lodestar of Australia, galvanising, informing, and dragging a generation or more into the magic and intricacies of science, its history, sociology and culture, and anointing it with excitement, humanity and wit. Not content with this varied and demanding diet as the tentacles of science unfurled, and keen to change the traditional picture of a scientist as a 'nerd' or 'the man in a long white coat', he drew every kind of science-connected person into his extending web: scientists in shorts, on the ground, in the sky and sea, casual laboratory scientists, informal high-fliers, women of every scientific range and kind. He regenerated and transmuted the very image of science and its life in Australia and overseas.

The Australian Broadcasting Commission claims a world leadership role in science for its weekly radio sessions of 'The Science Show', 'Ockham's Razor' and more. In 1989, goaded by those who said there weren't enough articulate Australian scientists to maintain a TV series in this country, Robyn Williams launched his multidisciplinary program 'The Uncertainty Principle' with a bang. It drew in the famous astronomer Robert Hanbury Brown, palaeontologist Michael Archer, immunologist Bede Morris, philosopher Peter Singer, nuclear physicist Sir Ernest Titterton, political scientist Don Aitkin, and – with a clear gender signal – the anti-nuclear advocate Helen Caldicott, two prominent Melbourne biologists Adrienne Clarke and Nancy Willis, and me, a science historian. The enthusiastic response to his program served to prove Robyn's point that Australian scientific research and intellectual life could be 'up there with the best' and it ran for ten more years. For me, this hour-long television exposure proved an invaluable turning point. Receiving enthusiastic feedback at a time when professional women were still battling to make their distinctive way, I emerged from it with a new confidence and authority – a sense of legitimacy that I had at last arrived! For this I owe Robyn deep gratitude. For there is no doubt that in our patriarchal society, women were and are still encultured to have lower self-esteem.

CHAPTER 11

THE AUSTRALIAN ARK

Historians do not always choose their own subjects. As Simone de Beauvoir observed: 'We cannot arbitrarily invent projects for ourselves, they have to be written in past requirement. 'Yet Eleanor Dark's comment was more precise. 'The past', she wrote with wide perception, 'coils like a spring and waits behind you to reach over your shoulder and join up with the future'. It might then be pertinent to ask what made me as a historian captive to the Australian ark?

Sometime in 1999, the resourceful science editor of Australia's leading publisher Allen & Unwin, Ian Bowring, called on me in Canberra. He wanted to know if there was a subject growing out of the history of Australian science that might contain some of the ingredients of Dava Sobel's best-selling book *Longitude*. With its intriguing mix of intertwining topics – the invention of the chronometer; the thrust of innovation and conflict; and the fierce ambitions of Britain's leading eighteenth-century scientific men – her story was attracting thousands of readers around the world. I believed there was. It was the story of Australia's extraordinary monotreme the platypus *(Ornithorynchus anatinis)*, and how this paradoxical creature, with its blend of reptile, bird and fur, had baffled international biologists and comparative anatomists in Britain and Europe for nearly ninety years. Moreover, in that great nineteenth century of scientific classification and advance, the strange Australian animal had challenged scientific knowledge in the northern hemisphere and confounded the established system of taxonomy.

Historians have something to bring to such themes. I had touched broadly on the platypus story in my documentary history *Scientists in Nineteenth Century Australia*, and again in '*A Bright & Savage Land*'. But now I found myself closely engaged with the story of an animal whose saga embraced a pre-eminent scientific fraternity; professional rivalry and conflict; a world audience; growing Australian research and knowledge; the Aboriginal people; and the striking discovery that, far from the platypus being a 'primitive' animal which, well into the twentieth century both British and Australian scientists affirmed, it was an animal whose strategies for survival in a competitive evolutionary environment would reveal it as one of the most sophisticated inhabitants of the animal kingdom.

Full of serendipitous turnings, a historian's route requires a deep scrutiny of the documentary sources; specific knowledge (in this case of the scientific mode of nineteenth-century science, its publications and differing voices); and an understanding of the historical participants. It is also open to the chance winds that blow an old article, an obscure long-forgotten paper, or a rare illustration into one's collecting bag. And here the platypus story, rich in its intertwining threads, would prove an absorbing detective hunt.

When the first platypus specimen reached England in 1799 it was seen as a colonial prank. But after the most minute and rigorous examination, Dr George Shaw, the British Museum's foremost naturalist, reluctantly conceded that this was no hoax, but 'a new and singular genus' whose form defied all current classification. Three key questions confronted the bemused biologists. Did this odd animal with the bill of a duck, webbed feet and a body swathed in fur, possess mammary glands and nourish its young with milk, and thus proclaim itself as a mammal? Did it, like other respectable mammals, give birth to live young? Or did it, like a bird, lay eggs or, like some reptiles, retain and hatch its young from eggs inside its body before expelling them alive? The answer was critical, for only the resolution of these crucial questions would allow this antipodean conundrum to be shoe-horned into the northern-hemisphere system of taxonomy and solve the riddle from across the world.

High flyers jostled on an international stage. In Britain there were the pre-eminent comparative anatomist at London's Royal College of Surgeons Sir Edward Home, and the younger, rapidly rising zoologist and comparative anatomist Richard Owen. Across the Channel, France's celebrated trio of biological professors Geoffroy St-Hilaire, Georges Cuvier, and Jean-Baptiste Lamarck were eagerly at work at Paris' Museum of Natural History. There was also the emerging German comparative anatomist Johann Meckel in the ring. Additionally, far distant in Australia, searching out specimens of the secretive animal to send for examination to experts 'at home', was Owen's close friend and one-time colleague, the British-trained naturalist Dr George Bennett, and the indigenous people who knew many of the answers.

Everard Home led the field with his illuminating verdict in 1802 that the platypus bill was not part of the animal's mouth, but rather an exploratory organ for touching and tasting used underwater in place of sight and smell. A year later the flamboyant Geoffroy St-Hilaire, securing a specimen from Australia, grouped the platypus with the echidna (which had arrived in England and Europe a few years earlier) and placed them together in a new taxon which he called 'Monotremata', denoting animals who used one orifice for both excretory and gestation purposes (known colloquially in Australia as 'one-holers'). Lamarck, however, protested that the platypus was neither bird nor reptile, and also not a mammal as it had no mammary glands. Rather, he placed the platypus with the echidna in a new class in the hierarchy of the animal kingdom which he named *Prototheria*, a taxonomic classification that persists to the present day. More than a decade later – for understanding marched in leisurely steps – France's high-priest of zoology Georges Cuvier tentatively placed the platypus and echidna with sloths and anteaters but advised that discussion of their method of generation could best be settled by those who observed the living animal in the field.

And so it continued until 1832 when, some thirty years after the platypus' landfall in Britain, Richard Owen, securing a number of well-preserved specimens from the colonies and aware that Meckel had identified primitive milk glands in the animal (opening without nipples onto its abdomen), proudly announced from careful dissection that both the platypus and echidna should be classed with the milk-nourishing mammalia. 'Not so!' shouted Geoffroy St-Hilaire with true French brio from across the Channel, 'If these are mammary glands where is the butter?'

Fascinated, I followed 'the paper war' that had thrust the platypus to the centre of international debate. This was new territory to me. I also tracked George Bennett's determined efforts to discover the method of platypus generation in the field. For this key question remained hotly contested. Both Geoffroy and Lamarck believed that the animal laid eggs. Meckel judged that the young might be born alive, while Owen, from his ready access to specimens and his skilled dissections, advanced the view that the platypus hatched its young from eggs within its body and was, as the word denotes, 'ovoviviparous'. Since his colleague George Bennett could find no eggs in his search among the labyrinthine platypus burrows and was willing to ignore the Aborigines' picturesque testimony that 'old woman have eggs there in so many days' and the young ones 'tumble down', it was a view that both he and Owen shared, and one that would delay resolution of the platypus puzzle for another fifty years!

Researching widely, I was rewarded to find my 'scientific polestar', Charles Darwin, among the players. Strangely his insights had been overlooked. Yet on his journey to the Blue Mountains that hot January of 1836, as the *Beagle* lay in Sydney Harbour, he had joined a platypus hunt one evening on the Cox's River and sent off a lively note to Phillip Parker King to record how splendid it was to be present at the killing of 'the wonderful animal'. Clearly Darwin had no knowledge of the animal's birth habits but, back in England as he pondered the aberrance and geographical distribution of species he had observed around the globe, the Australian platypus lingered in his mind. I followed his discussion in his correspondence with his colleagues Joseph Hooker and Charles Lyell, and turning to *The Origin of Species*, found that he described the *Ornithorynchus* as 'a living fossil' and 'a staunch survivor'. For Darwin, the platypus was like a pebble cast in a quiet pool, and when in 1874 he published *The Descent of Man*, it rose again as an exemplar of natural selection down to man.

But it was not until the 1880s, when the great evolutionist had been buried with honour in Westminster Abbey, that a bright young Scottish embryologist William Caldwell, trained as a

Darwinian at Cambridge University, arrived in Australia in 1884 on a British scholarship and, rounding up hundreds of platypuses on Queensland's Burnet River with the help of Aborigines, shot a female whose first egg 'had been laid' and whose second egg, he recorded, was 'in a partially dilated mouth of the uterus'. Off went Caldwell's famous telegram to British biologists meeting in Montreal that year which read simply: 'Monotremes oviparous, ovum meroblastic' (meaning the platypus laid soft-shelled eggs that held a large amount of food yolk). It was a message, transmitted by cable across the oceans, that made biological history. 'Who would have thought', the disappointed George Bennett opined to his friend Owen, both old men now, 'that an animal with so large a milk gland should actually demean itself by laying small white eggs!'

My step-by-step detective hunt had proved enthralling. I would follow 'my animal' across another century as platypus research shifted to Australia. Yet how secretive this creature was! Key embryological findings on the platypus egg would emerge from J. T. Wilson's youthful Department of Anatomy at Sydney University with its talented band of young researchers, Darwinians all. But it was not until the mid-1990s that Australian academics made the remarkable discovery of 'electro-reception' in the platypus bill that enabled it – with its eyes, ears and nostrils tightly shut – to avoid obstacles and locate its food when diving under water. Now the 'electric platypus' hit the world media once more. And as a fossil jaw of a large platypus ancestor was wrenched from the Cretaceous deposits at Lightning Ridge, New South Wales, the platypus emerged as the oldest living mammal in Australia with a lineage of more than 100 million years. It was, as Australia's platypus expert Mervyn Griffiths averred, 'the animal of all time'.

My book *Platypus*, subtitled *The Extraordinary Story of How a Curious Creature Baffled the World* was published in 2001, and attracted lively interest. Shortlisted for several national prizes, it went quickly into paperback; was reissued in America by the Smithsonian Institute in Washington and John Hopkins University Press; translated into Italian and Chinese; and stirred international attention. Thrillingly for a historian, it also yielded strong royalties. In effect, *Platypus* became something of a signature book.

There was more to come. This iconic animal became the first Australian mammal to be included in the famed United States Genome Project with its revolutionary new technology of genome sequencing. It was a high moment for Australian science when, following this, the Academy of Science held a conference in 2008 at Victor Harbour, South Australia, to celebrate and extend the findings. Along with the human, the Genome Project had already processed the genomes of a cluster of mammals, including the chimpanzee, the squirrel and the mouse. Now, findings on the platypus genome proved revolutionary. Here, conclusively identified, was the 'basal' evolutionary animal. Combining traits from three very different classifications, the platypus had survived down the great passage of evolutionary time when all other 'like' animals had gone to the wall. Hence, far from being an evolutionary accident, as long suspected, the animal emerged as 'a unique signature of evolution'; its genome revealed a clear fork in the evolutionary road some 166 million years ago when humans and other placental animals went one way and the platypus went another. It was, as one senior American biologist declared excitedly, 'our ticket of leave back in time'.

Off I went as its proud historian to join a multidisciplinary flock of microbiologists, chemists, embryologists, evolutionists, archaeologists, physicists, zoologists, ecologists, environmental scholars and many more drawn from around the world to apply my challenged mind to the intricacies of the new discoveries. They led in diverse, far-reaching directions. In response to my question as to the core message on the platypus' survival strategy, the senior French researcher replied with laudable simplicity, 'the message is in the milk'. Off I went to produce another chapter in a new edition of *Platypus* in 2010. But now a central new question has arisen. Can Darwin's 'great survivor' continue to adapt its survival strategies as human devastation heaps cumulative challenges on its pristine world? As early as 1990, Australian poet Judith Wright cast her elegiac eye on the platypus' familiar world.

> *Platypus, wary paradox,*
> *Ancient of beasts, like a strange word rising*
> *Through the waterhole's rocks,*
> *You're gone. That once bright water won't hold you now.*
> *No quick-silver bubble-trail*
> *In that scummy fetor.*
>
> *Under the banks' worn grass.*
> *No warm summer day*
> *Would bring a girl to watch*
> *That current pass*
> *For your wild shy head.*
>
> *The pool runs thick*
> *With car-bodies, cans, oil.*
> *The river's dead.*

We are its protector now.

THE KOALA

Protection, indeed, lies at the heart of the stories of Australia's two most famous faunal icons, the platypus and the koala. Soon after *Platypus*' appearance, I was invited to take up another sortie into the Australian Ark. But my resistance ran deep. One venture into this faunal arena of science's cultural history was surely enough! Moreover, the benign if quizzical koala offered a very different story from the platypus. It posed no burning classificatory puzzle; there was no contesting scientific cast of characters; it had inhabited this country through drought and ice age for some 33 million years, and its very physiognomy, the forward-looking face and sloping nose (unlike the pointed profiles of other mammals), was especially endearing to our human kind. Why take it on? Yet there were lively and important elements in its story. Twice the koala's survival has been at stake, but it had been brought back to safety ultimately through the power of literature (a striking story in itself) to secure an entrenched place in the national psyche, in the broad Australian culture, and in the national economy itself. Its story also seemed to bring to mind something of Mark Twain's artful observation on Australian history in his *Following the Equator*, written after he visited this country in the late nineteenth century. 'It does not read like history', he wrote there, 'but like the most beautiful lies. It is full of surprises, and adventures, and incongruities, and contradictions, and incredibilities; but they are all true, they all happened!'

So, after making a tentative survey of the research material, I was hooked. Surprisingly, tucked away in their high eucalyptus treetops, the koalas had remained publicly unknown to white settlers in Australia for some twenty-five years after settlement. Then, in 1803, a group of Aborigines brought two live koalas from the Illawarra district into the Sydney settlement. And there, by historical coincidence, the young British botanist-cum-zoologist on Matthew Flinders' *Investigator* voyage of Australia's circumnavigation Robert Brown, and the natural-history illustrator Ferdinand Bauer, became the first to define and accurately depict these curious and inconspicuous creatures. Paradoxically, in the severe loss of an official record, neither Brown's detailed 'type' description spelled out in Latin in that distant land, nor Bauer's scientifically precise and elegant illustrations, reached the public eye until late in the twentieth century.

Rather, it fell to the early colonial artist John Lewin, commissioned by Governor King, to provide a pictorial representation of the unknown animal which, reproduced in London's natural history journal *Arcana* in 1811, was met with deep disdain. 'As Nature provides nothing in vain', the naturalist George Perry observed bleakly, 'we may suppose that even these torpid, senseless creatures are wisely destined to fill up one of the great links of the chains of animated nature, and to show the extensive variety of created beings which God has, in his wisdom, constructed'. Perry consigned the koala broadly to the family of sloths. It was the young French zoologist Henri de Blainville, working in Paris several years later on his doctoral thesis on Australian monotremes, who rescued the animal and introduced a new generic specific for the koala, *Phascolarctos* from the Greek 'phaskolas' for leather bag (pouch) and 'arktos' meaning bear. The 'bear' stuck.

Fortunately for the koala, the Aboriginal people (for whom the koala was a significant figure in their 'Dreaming' stories) had struck a long environmental bargain with the animal to ensure the species did not come to harm. But it was destined for a chequered history in colonial Australia. The rapid reduction of koala habitat through land clearing in the nineteenth century was soon followed by the savage assault on the harmless creature by trappers, hunters and some graziers who made rich pickings in the export of koala fur. My research soon took on a disturbing edge as my sources revealed the brutal methods of koala killings. Keen for rapid action, hunters and trappers placed poison at the foot of eucalyptus trees and frequently stripped the animal of its fur while still alive, careless to the sight of a koala's piteous attempt to climb, naked, back up its tree. There was scant government protection. In 1902, 600,000 koala skins were recorded as purchased in New South Wales alone. One million koalas were slaughtered for their skin in Queensland in one official period for 'hunting bears' from April to September 1917, while by 1924 more than two million koala pelts were estimated to have left Australia. Only by 1927 did public protest halt the massacre.

It was Norman Lindsay's witty, 1918 book *The Magic Pudding*, with its endearing cast of characters – the sturdy koala Bunyip Bluegum, his travelling companions Bill Barnacle the sailor, Sam Sawnoff the penguin, and the raucous little 'cut and come' Pudding Albert – which eventually won hearts and secured a strong popular concern for the koala among Australians young and old. Never out of print, the book has remained an enduring classic and anchored the small marsupial in a favoured place in Australian society. Eager for my own close observation of the animal – for, like the early settlers, I had found koalas very difficult to see in their bush habitat – I paid a visit to Sydney's Taronga Zoo Park and, given privileged access, was introduced to a neat, well-behaved steel-grey koala called 'Norman' sitting out his period on display. 'Rather a curious name for a koala', I murmured to the young keeper of mammals. His reply was crisp. 'I christened him Norman', he said (having reared the koala from infancy when his mother cast him from her unmaternal pouch), 'after the artist Norman Lindsay who did so much for koala conservation'.

Plunging into the koala's biology and behaviour – the animal with the smallest brain in the mammal kingdom and the largest caecum (outer stomach) for its infinitely slow digestion of its special eucalyptus diet – my research grew. 'A man', as Samuel Johnson observed, 'will turn over half a library to make one book'. True for this woman. My research had given rise to a truly monumental pile of papers.

Late in my biographical journey, I had the pleasure of meeting the contemporary koala cartoonist Patrick Cook. Cook's weekly column on national life and politics, published in *The Bulletin*, had long offered a signature depiction of a small angry koala with a pen clenched firmly between its teeth. A latter-day Norman Lindsay with a sharper view, Cook perceived the national favourite as a singularly sardonic and savage little beast. Filling his collected works of koala cartoons with masterly sketches, he offered a highly confrontational little animal, protective of its trees disfigured by the crude marking of human hearts, and buoyantly obstructive to the crowding presence of *homo sapiens*. Cook's belief was explicit: '*We* think we're looking at them', he observed, 'but *they* are looking at *us!*' I cherish his thought.

Down its long evolutionary history, the koala had been seen in all States of Australia except Tasmania, which it was unable to reach across the swampy adjoining land. Its position, however, has now changed. Accelerating human development has significantly eroded the animals' scattered habitat, while the fierce 'wildfires' that now sweep the Australian landscape with devastating speed and heat are having critical impact on koala populations. Variously ranked as 'isolated', 'declining', 'vulnerable', 'endangered', 'extinct' in some areas, or 'stable', and on some off-shore islands 'in pest proportion', the Commonwealth Minister for the Environment in April 2012 at last formally listed the koala as 'vulnerable' in Victoria and New South Wales.

There have been prescient men. As long ago as 1871, Gerard Krefft, the far-sighted zoological curator of the Australian Museum, noted in his *The Mammals of Australia* that 'the koala has survived against the odds'. These odds have dramatically sharpened. Will the Australian koala, with its now deeply rooted connotations, manage to survive another century? We would be wise to embrace the message of that other far-sighted more recent protector David Fleay, who little more than a decade ago reminded us: 'May we never forget that their [the koala's] survival depends entirely on us'.

My book *Koala. A Historical Biography*, was published as a small, elegant volume rich in Bauer's depictions, by CSIRO Publishing in 2008. It never, however, received the plaudits that *Platypus* won. But such are the swings and roundabouts of a writer's work. In December 2008, I am eating my breakfast while reading the *Australian Book Review*'s list of selected authors' favourite books from 2008. There, British biographer Richard Holmes, in Australia that year to give the Seymour Lecture on Biography, had chosen the two works he admired. I read with approval his choice of Jill Roe's monumental biography of Miles Franklin. But can it be true? His second choice was my *Koala. A Historical Biography*. 'A miniature witty gem of a book', he suggests with his wondrous economy of phrase, 'which somehow gives us a compressed history of the entire country as seen from tree-top, leaf-nibbling level'. My day shone bright with reassurance!

CHAPTER 12

'THE BOTTOM LINE'

Who would not wish to have a sister? It is rightly claimed, notably by women, that a sister is the one person in your life you will probably know for longer than any other. Writing in 1814 in *Mansfield Park*, Jane Austen framed a more penetrating connotation. 'Children of the same family, the same blood, with the same first associations and habits', she observed, 'have some means of enjoyment in their power, which no subsequent connections can supply'. Whatever the circumstance – for change and transience are always there – the core blood-link binds forever. For me, my sister marked a crucial figure in my life.

Christened Mary Beatrice Hurley, but always called Mim or Mimi, she was the eldest of three children. Growing to become a tall, willowy stick of a girl with long arms and legs, a rounded face, perfectly sketched eyebrows, feet on ground, she was an individual from the start. My mother had pushed acorns into the ground outside our childhood's home on Sydney's lower North Shore and oak trees adorned the suburban nature strip. Mimi circled the leafy suburb on her bicycle, made friends in unlikely places ('not quite our kind' the murmur went) and offered shafts of wit. 'Miss Mothball I presume', she would remark when I, a 'goody goody', emerged in my carefully preserved winter clothes. Our younger brother, David, she adored.

My father, John Hurley, a gentle Catholic, and Doss, my mother (who, having converted briefly, had returned to her native Anglicanism after a brush with an uneducated priest), poured their loving attention equally down on us. And there, in our suburban home at Northbridge, we enjoyed a happy upbringing marked by the usual play and tiffs of childhood. When, in a nostalgic moment, Mimi and I revisited our Northbridge house in recent years, we found the acorn trees gone and the suburban house perceptively smaller than we recalled. Its value (my father having bought it in the 1930s for a thousand pounds) had extravagantly escalated to over a million dollars, and we realised wryly that we could never 'buy back the farm'! From our shared memories of that carefree childhood, however, our lives had shaped along differing lines.

Yet, who would choose to be the eldest child? Discarded unexpectedly from the single glow of parental attention, sidelined by the arrival of a younger sibling (for Mimi, when she was two), such children fashion different attitudes and achieve their first hard youthful adaptation to circumstance. Even so, the first in line acquires a certain enduring status. Mimi became the person who held the meaning of kin and family dear. In nature we were far apart, she conspicuously more practical, considerably less impulsive (more sensible), and decidedly less ready than I to take risks on human kind. Her happiness peaked when, in 1937, she went off to North Sydney's private girls' school 'Wenona', which Edith Ralston had established in 1920, naming it from a romantic fondness for the 'tall and slender maiden' of Longfield's *Story of Haiwatha*, but giving it a purposeful motto 'Ut Prossim' – that I may serve.

There, while not among the top scholars, Mimi found unanticipated rapport with the plump, formidable headmistress not known for bestowing attention and kindness on the average girl. I, by contrast – appearing two years later, good at school work, shy and diligent – Miss Ralston plainly disliked. For Mimi, her experience implanted an abiding respect for the importance of private education and a deep affection for the school that remained with her all her days.

In the custom of the period, she left Wenona after the Intermediate Certificate at the age of fifteen and went to work at the headquarters of the Commonwealth Bank, my father's place of work. It was the beginning of a career that, building diversely over time, would project her to a pioneering role on the Australian Stock Exchange.

Our sisterly lives, intermeshing across the war years – Mimi as an enthusiastic VAD (volunteering to support the war effort) and I as an Arts student at university – underlined our separate ways. I would come to know my sister best in specific interludes across our lives. Our sibling closeness grew when I left for England to take up my scholarship at London University in 1949 and she, catching my eager enthusiasm for the country and its war-torn city, followed within a year. Then we enjoyed halcyon youthful days living in a large Hampstead house with other Australian voyagers, those 'coming and going girls' who had arrived in England for short working periods and were off to the Continent or to hitchhike around Britain. 'Where are you off to this weekend?' English friends would slyly ask, 'Land's End or John o' Groats?' And off, never quite knowing, dependent on passing lifts, we would go.

Mimi put down her working roots in the Travel Section of the Bank of New South Wales in Berkeley Square, a glamorous, gossiping place in the 1950s. Batches of young Australian women crowded its rooms planning routes and excursions, making friends and connections, and building a lively corps who would scatter like eager birds over the beckoning world. Most of this roving feminine coterie returned to Australia to marry and produce children with young men who, in those early postwar years, took up jobs at home rather than venturing overseas. But neither Mimi nor I were the breeding kind. We were birds of another colour, destined to mark dead ends on the family and evolutionary tree. Quite soon, eager to maximise her administrative experience, she left the nightingales in Berkeley Square and returned to Sydney.

Though clearly not maternal, I was the marrying kind and had soon succumbed to an appealing Englishman, Michael Cousins, a wartime Ghurka officer and former tea planter whom I married for his very Englishness, his pipe-smoking handsomeness and charm. Not surprisingly, I soon decided that such settled niceness was not suited to my craving for an intellectual life and I became 'a bolter'. But I quickly launched into a second marriage to an atypical British army colonel, Everest Mozley, met on a long distance flight from London to the USA. That union lasted a brief thirteen months and I was 'out', nursing both pain and pique. And it was then that Mimi, returning to London from travel work in Canada, came to my aid and rescue. We would journey together at weekends to roam the English countryside, visit the grand castles that financially strapped aristocrats were opening to the public, enjoy lunch in a picturesque old pub and clamber aboard a Green Line bus back to London with our spirits lifted by exercise, kinship and air. It was then that I found my sister's sense of family and close support a reinforcing and precious gift. Restored, I stayed in England ready to return to my professional career while Mimi sailed back to Sydney.

It was at this point that her career in Australia shaped into distinguished form. I'll tie the pieces together. From the late 1950s, as Mary Hurley, she built a large reputation with her organisational and financial skills joining North & North, the first firm of stockbrokers to set up business in Sydney and Melbourne buying and selling options for clients. Mimi then became the second person to deal in options on the Australian Stock Exchange and from 1967 the first woman to be allowed to work as an operator on Sydney Stock Exchange's exclusively male floor.

She soon attracted press attention. 'The Stock Exchange, like the Roman Catholic Church', said Sydney's *Daily Mirror* bracingly in a lead article on 'Women in Business', 'has a traditional distaste for women in high places'. But while St Paul had yet to be flouted, 'the Sydney Stock Exchange has made a few exceptions to the rule'. One of these, they editorialised, 'is Mary Hurley who has the distinction of being the only woman options operator in Australia authorized to deal on the trading floor ... Tall, slim and in her early forties, she makes no concession to the mincing coyness usually associated with women in a predominantly male arena. She has a straight-forward, humorous manner and an obvious enthusiasm for her work'.

Her success in this highly professional and sophisticated arena of the Securities business gave me much pleasure even though, in my London Beaverbrook days, we were geographically far apart. She had, I knew, a strict work ethic that would have made her a valuable performer in this challenging field. 'Unless a person is efficient he is useless', she was reported as saying in interview in 1968. 'If he is efficient then most other things fall into place'. Miss Ralston would have been proud! My sister's strengths linked accuracy, reliability in decision-making, and sound business risk-taking, with a clear skill in building personal contacts with buyers. Her fascination with options provided a challenging and exciting career in which 'speed', she said, 'was the essence and any let-up of concentration can cost you dearly'.

Nonetheless it was tough going for a female operator pioneering in this determinedly masculine field. Inside the firm the fraternity gave no leeway. But she proved a drawcard for clients. Male colleagues 'either loved or hated me', she recalled. 'A couple of them would try to set me up if they were trying to offload stock'. But at the end of the day they would all troupe off together to the Wentworth Hotel for a friendly drink. She would ply this professional route at North's for twenty years, consolidating a large and valuable library of personal contacts.

It was at North's that Mimi met Judith Ryan, a strikingly pretty woman, a graduate in Arts from Sydney University, interested in music and the Italian language and working as a broker's research assistant. And so began a deep and lasting companionship, a friendship between two very different women whose life together harmonised their separate parts. Living abroad, I was unalert to the nature of her changing scene, and correspondence shed no light. But the fault-line in my sisterly relationship would rupture suddenly in 1971.

Returning to Australia from America that January to take up my first academic post at Sydney's New State Wales Institute of Technology (while Joe, at the top of his profession, awaited a promised professorship to follow me), I arrived at Sydney Airport late one Saturday night after an endless flight from Chicago. Having declined official overtures to meet me I was looking forward eagerly to finding my sister waiting for me. There was no one there. Rather there was a great emptiness. Baffled, I took the long taxi drive to Collaroy where Mimi lived with our widowed father. And it was then that I heard that she and Judith had set off happily together that morning on a driving holiday. I had much to learn. We had been separated by distance for several years; now, clearly, I was no longer central to her life. The difference of our predispositions was also plain. I was interested in men; Mimi had found her life's partnership with a woman. The very context of our lives had changed. Henceforward, I would not manage a close family conversation with my sister for forty years. There was now a close feminine duo – for me, an unforseen difference in this important respect from the usual partnered way.

But my sister had found true happiness. For many years the two women occupied their own apartments in an inner northern Sydney harbourside suburb, Mimi's with its high, spanning view of Sydney Harbour, and Judith's a gardened enclave in a nearby street. Thereafter, they spent their treasured leisure time together and embarked on those travelling excursions at home and overseas that became a hallmark of their enmeshed lives. Fortune tellers marked their futures and fortune with tinkling bells. They heard them in many Asian countries, developed an avid taste for Virginia Woolf and her writings, pursued her homes in England and set their course for journeying around Britain, Greece and Europe.

The floodgates, however, burst open on their security on 'Black Monday', 19 October 1987, when the world shuddered at the sudden, seemingly inexplicable drop in the world stock markets that signalled the largest one-day percentage decline in stock market history. By the end of the month the Australian Stock Market had fallen by forty-one per cent, the second severest in world decline – almost double that of Britain and the United States. No major events or news foreshadowed this disastrous crash, but markets around the world went on to restricted trading as sorting orders overwhelmed the existing computer technology. Then women employees were the first to go. Judith, clearing her desk on the Friday after the crash, made her way unnoticed down the firm's back stairs. And despite her expertise and knowledge, Mimi followed some weeks later, while less adept or experienced male staff (for were they not 'the family wage earners'?) were retained. Masculine survival was the bottom line; Mimi's invaluable library of contacts passed to their hands. It was a savage assault for both women but more potent for my sister with her long experience and renown.

They fell into unexpected poverty, climbing out of it by working at Christmas as mail sorters at the GPO; joining a vegetable cannery in rural Batlow, and surviving a medley of lowly jobs in Sydney where it was necessary to be respectful to young male bosses. Professional openings in finance disappeared. Mimi, stronger and more capable than her friend, carved out a joint existence for them. Joe and I were their nurturing friends.

Yet the role of two closely linked women posed challenges in this period. They were socially on the edge. They fiercely rejected any styling as 'lesbians'. It did not fit their ways. They reminded me evocatively of that classic book *The Ladies of Langollen. A Study in Romantic Friendship*, which I had read with lively interest in my early days in England relating the story of two upper-class women from Northern Ireland, Eleanor Butler and Sarah Ponsonby, who, resisting the prospective 'marriages of arrangement' made by each of their families, had eloped to live together in a house in Wales. Linked for fifty-one years, they were buried side by side with their faithful maid.

Mimi and Judith's affection for each other became their life's strong bond. During the 1990s they moved together into a sun-filled apartment close to Wenona where my sister had become a benefactor and where she enjoyed the passing contact made with 'Wenona girls'. Linked lovingly to kin, nieces and nephews and an emerging generation of Judith's 'grands', the two remained in part an enclave, contented, but obliged to adopt ways of living different from traditional partnered lives.

They often visited Canberra to stay with me, delighting in the beauty and culture of the capital. Sisters, as the gathering literature tells us, are variously 'loving', 'independent', 'critical', 'estranged for periods', 'protectors' and 'the loyalest of supporters in troubled times'. These experiences we shared. I knew the 'In and Out Club' well. Mimi did not always approve of me and at times I felt that I had lost a sister. Drusilla Modjeska, in her edited book *Sisters*, had expressed it well: 'the complicated, uneven tide of lived feelings that passes between girls who share parents: sensitivity to slights and differences, and love as abiding as blood'.

My sister and I grew closer as bad health and dementia overtook Judith in more recent years and Mimi came to spend time on respite leave with me, alone. How warm and strengthening it was then to talk freely about our concerns and, without another's presence, to reminisce. She was becoming her most beautiful in older age, handsome and stylish while she actively assumed the role of family head. I was very proud of her. She, in turn, showed a deep interest in my professional life, working her way through my books, attending their launches with pride, supporting me in Joe's increasing illness, an encourager and my calming friend. But she kept her own cards close to her chest.

So it was, late in November 2006, that I received an early evening telephone call from a Sydney vascular surgeon telling me that he had examined my sister by angiogram that day and had introduced a stent in her leg. 'I have saved her life', he said, 'but I may have to amputate'. I was overcome with horror. For I had no notion that a sore foot which she had mentioned a month before, as we wandered among the flowers of Canberra's Floriade, was more than a discomfort, perhaps a serious corn. Now my elegant sister, misdiagnosed and neglected by her Sydney doctor and neglectful of her own health while caring for her friend, had been found with gangrene in her foot and would, in all probability, lose her leg. Shock, terrible pain and pity – for 'pity, beyond all telling', writes Sally Vickers, 'is hid in the heart of love' – were my portion. I drove to Sydney.

She was very 'Mimi-ish' in those next weeks in hospital. Her personality flowed. She was surrounded by Judith's nieces, their daughters and their mother. Chatter and laughter filled the air. Flowers spilled over. She greatly enjoyed her early-morning exchanges with the nurses, though she had her preferences. Several of her toes were turning black; dressed daily and looked at by doctors, they remained menacing, and uncured. If she was in pain she did not show it. With her soft curled hair and fine complexion, her very presence gave pleasure. I would hear her phrase 'the bottom line' in those December weeks. Drawn from her financial background, it became something of a mantra, a signature statement in her sentences, meaning at times the fundamental point, the final measure of competence, the last word. 'The bottom line', she would say to me expressively, her finely shaped eyebrows rising, 'is such and such'. But from the medicos there were no spoken bottom lines.

My brother, David, and I, dissatisfied with the casual medical and nursing attention in the private hospital, arranged for her to move by ambulance to the Royal North Shore Hospital fronted by a competent gerontologist. I waited in my car outside the private hospital my engine ready to follow her transport, tears streaming down my cheeks. Yet she took great interest in the move and I found her buoyant in Emergency chatting and joking with the ambulance men. They placed her in a ward with three frail-looking old men. She did not appear to mind. Rather, she revelled in her cubicle's window that looked out towards the Harbour.

Even so, she longed for home. 'I must catch up with my work', she said. Her work, deeply rooted in her old professional life, was keeping strict and splendidly organised records of her shares and business affairs. It gave her focus, an imperative call. Her other deep concern was that she should be with Judith, now terminally ill with cancer, when she died. But there was no more talk of amputation. It was as if the doctors, confronted, had merely decided to let it rest. Late one afternoon, now poisoned by infection, she looked at me and said, 'I love you', and turned to sleep. On urgent advice, we moved her to a spacious flower-filled room in a private hospital for hospice care.

Rushing about all my life, I had expected to predecease my sister and had once urged her, 'Promise me you will sit beside me when I am dying and chat to me. Don't let my quiet friend M. sit wordless for I have no wish to go silent into "the long silence"'. 'Yes', she said, 'I will'. Now the tables were abruptly turned. For two days of her unconscious, morphine-easing sleep, I sat beside her talking to her of shared happiness, our days past, and our times together as she battled her way to life's close. For Mimi the bottom line was death. Yet we had come together once more as the closest of sisters 'with love as abiding as blood'.

> *Ruined yet pure we go,* (wrote Judith Wright)
> *With all our days and deeds,*
> *Into that flame, that snow.*

Moving among her possessions, clearing their apartment, I find the full evidence of my presence in my sister's life – the framed photographs, my signed books, a portrait, gifts and remembrances of every kind. She had been 'the watcher of my ways' and I am overwhelmed by grief and love. But I did not own her. Judith, unaware and solitary, died four months later and their plaques to each other, chosen many years before, rest with their ashes side by side.

We know so little about the deep heart of each other across almost eighty years. But the year of 2007, while I worked on a biography of the koala, was, I know, the unhappiest of my life. We construct our own bulwarks and patterns against loneliness and disappointment, but in my independent and committed life, it was no longer the professional component that lay at its core, but the profoundly personal. I reach for the phone and my sister is no longer there.

CHAPTER 13

WRITING 'MR CLARKE'

In all my years of research on the nineteenth century in Australia, a small handful of remarkable men have left an indelible stamp on my mind. But none, it can be said, more so than the geological Anglican clergyman the Rev William Branwhite Clarke. 'Mr Clarke' – as my husband would patiently call him – belonged to that long line of naturalists who filled the pages of my early books on nineteenth-century science. Through the care and thoroughness of his recording, he was destined to become my key witness and testator in the story of the rise of the Australian scientific community and its interconnection with science overseas.

Born in 1798 in East Bergholt, Suffolk, Clarke was a graduate of Cambridge University and had served in several English parishes when, in 1838, he accepted nomination to a chaplaincy in New South Wales. Many sons of the middle classes educated for the church at Oxford or Cambridge and, lacking the prospect of preferment in Britain, chose to come to fill Anglican parishes in the Australian Colonies; but William Clarke was different. He had attended, at Cambridge, the early geological lectures of Professor Adam Sedgwick ('hitherto I have never turned a stone; henceforth I will leave no stone unturned' was his winning inaugural cry); contributed papers on geological and meteorological subjects to British journals; and had been elected a Fellow of the prestigious Geological Society of London. Now he set out with his geological hammers, his theodolite, barometers and collecting bags, and the explicit intention of creating a 'new earth for geology' in Australia.

Clarke arrived in Sydney with his wife and two children in May 1839. Discerning a true intellectual, the Bishop of Australia at once appointed him for a year to the headmastership of The Kings School, Parramatta (which he had earlier established for the education of the sons of gentlemen) with charge of the neighbouring parishes of Dural and Castle Hill. Five years later Clarke became the first pastor of the new church of St Thomas', St Leonards (North Sydney) a post he held as a renowned and respected clergyman until his retirement in 1871.

What, then, made me choose this particular man for a work of scholarship that would occupy me for a decade or more from the 1990s to frame the story of a growing colonial scientific community? There are two answers. My sole training in science derived from my school years at Wenona, where I studied geology under the brilliant teacher – and Edgeworth David's one-time student – Nancy Grace. But the second and crucial reason lay in the fact that history, in its random way, had delivered me the Clarke Papers, deposited in the Mitchell Library of the State Library of New South Wales. These held the private correspondence of a rare communicator who, across his long career in New South Wales from 1839 until 1878, had built up an extensive correspondence with members of the scientific community within the colonies and key scientific figures around the world. In contrast, then, to other contemporary colonial naturalists a number of whom achieved distinction, Clarke alone had carefully preserved his correspondence and maintained it for posterity. Of the total of some 2,700 letters in his papers, an overwhelming number related to the geological and natural sciences and to the practice, context, methods, controversies, development and the community of Australian science. Setting his church correspondence aside, Clarke's scientific papers and the life they reflected hence became – in the words of another scientific editor – 'the thread on which the beads of history are strung'.

W. B. Clarke (for his initials early clung to him as his signifier) was also, as I quickly learnt, a 'maker and shaker'. He was hardly in Sydney more than a week – observing the gangs of convicts in their grey-flannel garments, the sparse network of streets in the city, and a forlorn Aboriginal family on the ferry to his area of placement at Parramatta – before he made contact with the proprietor of the *Sydney Morning Herald*, John Stokes. Through his writings on science and exploration he developed a sustained connection with successive editors of the newspaper, which came to be known informally as the 'scientific journal' of the Colony. With his letters of introduction from scientific men in Britain, Clarke was also rapidly in touch with members of the local scientific community – the Colonial Secretary and entomologist Alexander McLeay and his distinguished son, the zoologist William Sharp McLeay, himself a recent arrival from England; the Scottish astronomer at Parramatta Observatory James Dunlop, brought out by Governor Brisbane in 1821 to found the physical sciences in Australia; and the renowned navigator and meteorologist, native-born Phillip Parker King, who became his close friend. He was, too, soon out on his horse riding around Parramatta and Prospect, filling his collecting bags with fossils; for, as Charles Darwin had remarked on the *Beagle* voyage three years earlier, 'there is nothing like geology in finding a fine group of fossil bones which tell their story of former times with almost a living tongue'.

By December 1839, Clarke had also managed to meet the brilliant young geologist of the United States Exploring Expedition James Dwight Dana – destined to become the leader of that science in America – who had arrived in Sydney as a member of the expedition's scientific corps. Delighted and exhilarated by each other, the two men rode together through the rugged Illawarra countryside, examining the outcrops of Sydney sandstone along the coast and conducting researches that would form part of each of their early writings on the geology of Australia and cement a friendship that lasted all their lives.

Scientific investigators of every kind faced daunting challenges in Australia. Those interested in botany or zoology met instant difficulties in the lack of comparative collections of specimens to aid them in their identification of the unique flora and fauna. And the rocks, fossils and structural character of the formations offered unanticipated problems for the pioneering geologist. Some isolated geological information had been gathered during maritime expeditions early in the nineteenth century. Baudin's 'geological gentlemen' made observations of rocks and landscape in 1802–3 largely from 'off shore', while Darwin, riding on horseback across the Blue Mountains in January of 1836, had set down his conclusions on the possible formation of the magnificent cliffs and valleys which he likened (erroneously) to the action of the sea. But in 1839, Australian stratigraphy was an open field.

Clarke had arrived in New South Wales with recent knowledge of the key formations and stratigraphy of Great Britain which geologists had been busily stitching together through the work of the Geological Survey of Great Britain, established in 1835. He had also learnt from the eminent leaders Adam Sedgwick and Sir Roderick Murchison and he was eager to apply this knowledge to unravelling the formations of Australia. Sedgwick gave his old pupil warm encouragement, urging him on the eve of his departure to the Antipodes to make the coal deposits the first priority of his research. 'I shall rejoice to be in correspondence with you', he wrote Clarke in December 1838. 'I wish you health, happiness, and success with all my heart'.

It was hence to Sedgwick that Clarke confided the complexities of his early fieldwork and to whom he sent his most-prized collections of fossils for identification at the Cambridge Woodwardian Museum. 'The difficulties are so great in this country to the Geologist', he was soon writing his old mentor, 'owing to the peculiar construction of the country, its deep and impassable ravines, its enormous forests, its want of crossroads, and good sections, it is only by most painful plodding, that one can make out anything satisfactory'. But plod he did, and by August 1840 his next letter was reporting: 'I have during the past year not been idle in the way of observation. I have explored the whole of the Illawarra as far as the Shoalhaven, the Kangaroo Grounds in the County of Cumberland, the Blue Mountains & the Coal district of the Hunter and the country along the Williams River up to Port Stephens & when my leisure allows I intend to lay a general account of this tract before the [Geological] Society'. Most importantly, Clarke was able to tell Sedgwick that he had found the whole of the lower strata of the coal rocks in these regions charged with fossils and had reached the conclusion that he was dealing, not with a young continent as had been long suspected, but with an immensely old land where the presence of silicified coniferous wood along with granite could be 'relics of the vegetation of the primitive granitic hills of ancient Australia'. By 1847 he was able to confirm, from his discovery of the ancient fossil Trilobites from the Protozoic rocks in southern New South Wales, the great geological age of Australian formations.

I followed him closely in his scientific correspondence transferring his decidedly challenging handwriting to typescript form. 'You were always diligent', my brother reminded me. This was true. But diligence is the style of the historian, and so I tracked my man. What a place the Colony was! Keenly curious about new discoveries, Clarke swiftly befriended the young inland explorers Ludwig Leichhardt and Edmund Kennedy, finding Leichhardt 'no common man' and highlighting his early inland expeditions in the press. In turn, Leichhardt dropped Clarke's name on a northern New South Wales river and, preparing to set out on his third, and fatal, expedition into the empty desert to carve a route overland to the west, wrote his clerical friend, 'Take care of my Barometer, and as you observe its gentle rise and fall, so imagine your friend's spirits rising and ebbing down during the daily progress of his enterprise'. With Leichhardt's disappearance with his entire party in 1848, it was Clarke who used his connections in the Sydney press to stir public interest in an official search and kept the torch bright in the Australian community for his discovery. He would act as a similar correspondent and reporter for the young surveyor Kennedy, whose exploratory journey in 1846 through the dense rainforest of northern Queensland resulted in his untimely death from an Aborigine's spear within sight of his naval rendezvous at Cape York.

Clarke's pen would also draw in the British naval captains engaged on British Admiralty survey around the Australian coast and their attendant naturalists – the geologist J. B. Jukes was one such, destined to make his reputation and professional place in Britain. Clarke befriended them in Sydney and garnered geographical and meteorological data from them, in correspondence, to fuel his writing for the Sydney press. After less than two years in New South Wales, he had made considerable headway. But life would bare its teeth. Clarke's wife Maria absolutely detested the Colony and its marks of a convict society, and despite the birth of a second daughter in 1841, she determined to leave Australia with the children to what she saw as the chance of a better education for their son in Britain. Hence, two-and-a-half years after their Australian landfall, on New Year's day 1842, Clarke stood on the cliff above Sydney Heads and watched his wife and three small children sail out of Sydney Harbour bound for his mother's home in Britain. He would not see them again for fifteen years.

Maria's departure, however, proved a gift to Australian science. Now a solitary figure, Clarke devoted his spare time to science, writing by candlelight at night in his quiet rectory or on excursions camping in the field, and spinning a spreading skein of correspondence that would open a window on the scientific and intellectual society of this country.

His own time for major expeditions would come later with the impact of Edward Hargreaves' 'discovery' of gold at Ophir in 1851. Tapping with his hammer around the rock formations near Hartley, New South Wales, Clarke had himself discovered traces of gold in 1841, sending the first miniscule export of the metal to his mother in England and calling on Governor Gipps at his Parramatta residence with his find. There he elicited the cry from the cautious governor of a convict colony (which schoolboys have treasured down the years), 'Put it away, Mr Clarke, or we shall all have our throats cut'! But Clarke did not 'put it away', and throughout the 1840s continued to prophesy Australia's potential gold and other mineral resources in the columns of the Sydney *Herald*. In mid-1851, freed temporarily by his Bishop from clerical duties, he accepted appointment from the New South Wales government to conduct a geological and mineralogical survey of the Colony, journeying on horseback with two assigned convict servants from his parish in North Sydney to Omeo at the southeast tip of New South Wales and back. Zigzagging across immense landscapes to carry the survey northwards to Ipswich in 1853 he travelled over a total distance of some 60,000 square miles. His small figure, for he stood at 5 foot 4, became a familiar sight at the diggings where his geological know-how was in high demand, and where he preached Christ's teaching as he searched the earth for the evidence of gold. As news of new mineral discoveries spread – through extracts from his detailed reports to government published in the Sydney press – the 'Rev. W. B. Clarke' became a household name.

The gold discoveries rapidly changed the character of the Australian colonies. As the early geological surveys began their somewhat fractured history in this country, Clarke made welcome contact with the young trained geologists arriving from Britain to conduct surveys in Victoria, Tasmania and Queensland. And in Clarke, the new recruits found an intellectual linchpin and vital sounding board. Their incoming letters (for Clarke's letters to them have not survived) catch at their friendship and need. Charles Gould, son of the ornithologist John Gould, arrived from Britain in 1859 to head the Geological Survey of Tasmania, and was soon off on a gold mission to that colony's southwestern mountains, dropping the names of British scientists 'Darwin', 'Huxley', 'Jukes' and 'Murchison' on the high-topped peaks. 'I have so few opportunities now of communicating ideas', he wrote Clarke eagerly, 'that any break in correspondence with yourself amounts to a very positive misfortune', while Richard Daintree, the young head of Queensland's Northern Geological Survey, cried out: 'Oh for a forty parson power to rouse the inert masses of slumbering politicians'. Later, Charles Wilkinson, appointed head of the New South Wales Geological Survey in 1875, would follow in Clarke's pioneering geological footsteps in the northern regions of New South Wales and prepare his *Geological Map of New South Wales* (1880 and 1882), embracing the knowledge of Clarke's many years of fieldwork and information he had gathered from his younger colleagues for posthumous publication.

The golden wealth of colonial governments also contributed to the rise early in the 1850s of the universities of Sydney and Melbourne. At Sydney, the young Dr Alexander Thomson, Reader in Mineralogy and Geology, and Archibald Liversidge, Professor of Chemistry, became Clarke's important friends. The two-way correspondence of Clarke and Thomson numbered some 70 letters, illustrating the close bonds he made with his young colleagues and their role in shaping new knowledge in the Colony.

At the same time, Clarke's international web stretched outwards. As soon as *The Origin of Species* reached Sydney in 1860, he was in touch with Darwin. While the first page of his congratulatory letter has been lost from the Darwin Papers at Cambridge, Clarke's words evidently offered warmth and keen geological cooperation. 'Your name has of course been familiar to me for years', Darwin replied in October 1861. 'I am very glad to hear of your new discoveries of Secondary fossils in N.S. Wales. I have for some time thought that the geology of distant countries would help in the progress of the Science more than anything else; and in this you have been an earnest worker. Most cordially do I wish you all success'. Clarke's personal position on evolution would remain two edged. Essentially, across his scientific career he was a 'uniformitarian' and evolutionist in geology who recognised the appearance and extinction of species over infinitely changing eras of geological time. But as a clergyman, like the eminent Dana in America and Britain's leading palaeontologist Sir Richard Owen, he remained a 'separate creationist' throughout his career.

Nonetheless, in his inaugural presidential address in 1867 to the Royal Society of New South Wales which he had helped found, Clarke publicly pressed his scientific contemporaries in the Colony to a clear and unbiased examination of all new scientific ideas. 'We must strive to discern clearly, understand fully, and report faithfully', he declared, 'to adjure hasty theories and unsupported conjectures; to give our brother observer the same measure of credit we take to ourselves leaving time for the judgment which will inevitably be given either for or against us'. At the same time he stressed the importance of attending to Australian discoveries: 'We have before us in this Colony a new heaven for Astronomy and a new earth for Geology ... We have facts to accumulate relating to Droughts and Floods. We have unrevealed magazines of mineral wealth in which Chemists and Miners will find employment for ages after we have mingled with our parent soil'. His vision soared.

W. B. Clarke's particular significance in the history of Australian science lay in the fact that he flourished at a time when science was the province of the independent investigator, but moving towards a new and growing professionalism. As an active participant, he played a major role. For amid his clerical christening, marrying, burying, offering Sunday services, and tending a far-flung flock, he managed to produce a swag of scientific books, geological papers published in British and Australian journals, and a stream of communications and letters on Australian scientific discoveries and exploration in the Sydney press. He classified the coal deposits of New South Wales and published a number of editions of his foundation study, *The Sedimentary Formations of New South Wales*. Professional delays inevitably hung about his work as the absence of comparative collections of specimens for the identification of his massive hauls of fossils left him, at times for several years, waiting for expert identification from overseas. In the event, his important collections of Palaeozoic and Carboniferous fossils were classified, not by British pundits, but by the Belgian palaeontologist Professor Laurent-Guillaume de Koninck at Liège, in a correspondence conducted entirely in French.

For half a century Clarke was the leading scientific savant in New South Wales. As the first President of the Royal Society of New South Wales, he sat at the centre of a growing scientific community. Many of the men involved in this new community had, before settling in Australia, served in diverse and responsible occupations around the world; it was a community that was cosmopolitan in its origin, informed, increasingly professional, and in touch with shifting international trends in science overseas. In this, Clarke's own life in science (and the correspondence it generated) contradicted the perception long purveyed by many senior historians of mainstream Australian history of 'the prevailing intellectual barrenness in the colonies'. In New South Wales, Clarke stood at its source and centre. Moreover, in a country that for many decades lacked a support system in science, his growing expertise on the Colony's resources of coal, gold, other minerals and artesian water, gave him direct access to governors, administrators and legislators, which allowed him key participation in the emerging relationship between government and science. His role in the public communication of science also attracted a wide correspondence from settlers, pastoralists, gold and mineral fossickers, interested scientific amateurs, and naturalists of every kind.

W. B. Clarke was a polymath. His nets never dried. At seventy-eight he had the pleasure of at last being elected a Fellow of the Royal Society of London. 'You have founded the geology of a continent and a Royal Society of your own', the political economist William Stanley Jevons (whom Clarke had known as a young man at the Sydney Mint in the 1840s) wrote him, as joint signatory with Charles Darwin of his election. The Clarke Medal of the Royal Society of New South Wales, the first scientific medal struck in Australia, was created in his honour following his death in 1878.

What a venture this work of scholarship had proved! To carry it out, I had won a half C. H. Currey Fellowship of the State Library of New South Wales, where aware of the vastness of the project, the library had lent me a staff member, Stephen Martin, to help with the initial sorting and transcription of the work. His short-time presence gave enormous fillip to the work. But in the long term, essentially I was on my own. The crucial task of selecting, transcribing, and referencing Clarke's correspondence from the papers and locating and drawing in his outgoing communications from other archives in Australia and overseas, was formidable. 'The footnotes alone', said my encouraging editor, 'would have made another book!'

Documentary undertakings such as this are traditionally carried out by a team of editors and researchers – the von Mueller collection in Australia, *Regardfully Yours: Selected Correspondence of Ferdinand von Mueller* edited by Rod Home, is such a one, involving international editorial collaboration and the aid of research assistants. Was it rashness on my part, to attempt the work alone? Yet once begun, the dye was cast. Gathering and transcribing some 898 letters, I had formed a deep attachment to the man. My acquaintance with him was intimate. I knew his hopes and aspirations, his dedication and fierce determination, his ambition and disappointments, his wide inclusiveness and generosity, his open support for young scientists, his worldly poverty, and the struggle as an independent scientist to obtain priority for his work. I also became attuned to the illnesses which from time to time crippled his already vexed handwriting. And when, unanticipated, I came upon a letter written by a visiting New Zealand geologist to a colleague across the Tasman that read 'We have buried the Rev. W. B. Clarke', my tears flowed. In a deep sense, Clarke's life had latched itself into mine. In Richard Holmes' ever evocative words, it had become 'a handshake across time'.

The Web of Science. The Scientific Correspondence of the Rev. W. B. Clarke. Australian Pioneer Geologist, in its massive 1,240 pages, was published in two volumes by Australian Scholarly Publishing in 2004. Viewing it, it appeared that no one of any relevance or importance – be they scientists, governors, jurists, explorers, surveyors, administrators, politicians, bureaucrats, meteorologists, key settlers, and a medley of scientific luminaries around the world – had failed to mark their presence, while a whole landscape of scientific investigation and cultural and community affairs had been revealed. Historians choose their own distinctive routes to knowledge. For me, it will always be the documents. In this work they lay at its core. Like a distant echo, the words of two French historians working together at the end of the nineteenth century ring in my ears *'Rien ne supplée aux documents: pas de documents, pas d'histoire'*. 'Nothing can replace documents: without documents, there is no history'.

The Web of Science was launched at the State Library of New South Wales by my friend and colleague, the nineteenth-century historian Don (D. W. A.) Baker, who had supported the project from the outset and had read every manuscript page. My debt to him was enormous as it was to two other key participants – my clever godson Angus Rea who devised and masterminded the elegant computer format for the work, and my publishing editor Dr Diane Carlyle, who became my vital colleague and friend. 'It has a great look', I remarked to Paul Brunton, head of the Manuscript Collections at the State Library of New South Wales, as I gazed with a mother's pride at the two earth-coloured volumes at their launch. 'But what about the contents', he exclaimed. 'It will furnish researchers for generations to come!'

Postscript.
In 2011, I go to meet a tall, sprightly man of ninety-three at Canberra Airport. They are making them taller these days. It is John Clarke flying in from Melbourne to visit me. In December 1856, W. B. Clarke's long-absent wife, Maria, and his three grown children, returned to Australia after fifteen years in Britain to join him – an outcome made possible by the generous sum which his parishioners at St Thomas' Church had raised after the partial stroke Clarke suffered in his pulpit on Easter Day. As a result, a large family of Clarkes, descending in his name from his son, Mordaunt, were dispersed in Australia. In recent years, when it was my custom to spend time with M. among a circle of friends

on Victoria's Mornington Peninsula, I would often encounter a tall figure who had served as an Australian pilot with the British Air Force in World War II, flying planes to the North African campaign. Handsome and alert, John Clarke looked the part. His British wife, whom he married at the war's end, had died and, now a widower, John was there in our company with his old-world charm and courtesy. But Clarke is a common name, and why mention one's work at social gatherings, or for that matter, one's lineage? When, however, a mutual friend saw *The Web of Science* on John Clarke's coffee table, she exclaimed: 'But that's Ann Moyal!' 'And I'm W. B. Clarke's great-grandson', was John's swift reply!

John Clarke has now become my rewarding friend. Invited each year by the headmaster of William Clarke College – the Anglican school established more than twenty years ago at Kerryville, Sydney, in Clarke's early parish of Dural – John Clarke and I walk together in the formal procession at the College's yearly prize-giving, where we link the bright new generation of College students to their historical past.

CHAPTER 14

'ONLY CONNECT'

'One hears the clock very loudly', said Australia's expatriate Clive James in an interview on the ABC, 'yet one is aware of the connections and interconnections with one's links in between'. I have never been a particular fan of Clive James, too egotistical, too maddeningly successful – but I applaud him for this resonant truth. For, if I were asked for my most favoured concept, after 'friendship' and 'love', I would choose 'connecting' and its sequence 'interconnection' (even while I deplore the increasing commercial and information-communication 'take-up' of these words). Yet, in their purest sensibility, they shape, surprise and enhance one's days. Ultimately, of course, they will lead one to a final connection. But ever since reading E. M. Forster's *Howard's End* in my impressionable girlhood, I have responded to its heroine's fevered cry, 'Only connect', and held it to me as a talisman.

I have been walking with my fifty-something friend Jenny on the beach at Bruny Island, the magical island off the south-east coast of Tasmania that sits, full of sombre and haunting history, like a glowing jewel. Such a deeply loved friend marks an essential truth for women: 'always make friends of younger women'. The sea blazes brilliant blue, small boats ride at anchor, and the pure, shallow-green water laps luminous at our feet as Jenny's sleek Weimaraner leaps joyously to retrieve a ball. Jenny came into my life by wondrous circling paths. Beautiful, full of intelligence and charm, she would be my daughter's age if I had ever paused to have a child. I met her when she was two years old, when her academic father, then a handsome, divorcing historian at the ANU (to whom after my return from Britain I was briefly in thrall), held her up at my office window – a tiny form with a crop of curly dark hair, a symbol of enticement. He was off to a post at an Asian university and his subsequent love letters, beckoning yet flexible, included her in my future world. 'Come to my new place of appointment [though pay your own fare it seemed to say], and stay'. But newly settled in Australia after nine years overseas, this was not part of my plan.

Forty years passed before I met Jenny again. Then, past and present mingled in their entwining ways when my friend M., a one-time colleague of her father's, took me to visit her in her Canberra home. Her own sophisticated, professional life in Europe had engrossed her but, returning to Australia with two young sons, she had married again to an Australian lawyer, and swam into my ken. Captured by Tasmania, she and her husband moved to Hobart. Yet across our sixteen years of friendship, stimulus, joy and laughter have mapped our ways. 'Intimacy at a distance', is the label I coined when, in my telecommunications days, I was researching and reporting on women and the telephone in Australia, for those long, personal telephone calls across distance on which women's happiness, self-esteem and comfort relied. With Jenny's move off the mainland, we form a part of this vital telephone linking chain.

Bruny Island, where she has built a house, now fills an important place in my affairs. Historically, it's of a piece. For there in February 1802, the naturalist François Peron landed, more than two centuries ago, as a member of France's exploring scientific expedition to Terra Australis, christening it with quiet enchantment as 'the rare extremity of the globe'. The resourceful Peron made contact with the island's indigenous people and one feels the presence of those Aboriginal ghosts in the cluster of native sand grasstrees *(Xanthorrhoea arenaria)* at the edge of Jenny's property that stretches down to the D'Entrecasteaux Channel. Alert to the success of the Writers' House at Varuna, my friend plans to transpose its concept to Bruny Island, and our discussions shape happily around the day when three writers will come through spaced fellowships each year to find inspiration in this creative place. Clearly I must ensure that I live long enough to see it flourish.

Some links across generations are tight from the start. Holidaying in Jakarta, I had met another of my close younger friends Margaret Pearce, a senior public servant, when M. (again ever a man of friendships) took me to stay with her and her journalist husband and she became my dear inheritance. 'Here', she told me later, 'I thought, is someone who could be a substitute for my mother' who had died some years before. The image was surprising for, as my literary alter ego 'Ann Veronica', was wont to cry, 'I'm not a good type of woman; there's something of the male in me!' Yet what manna her perception brought! Over the intervening years in Canberra, our closeness grew as we weathered those stormy, pressured times that flowed around high-placed public servants during Kevin Rudd's first Prime Ministership. Driving home at 7pm each evening after a near twelve-hour day, her journalist husband still at work, my friend would telephone me to, as she put it, 'dump her stress' and protect her young daughter from its burden. These conversations, lively among the traffic, yielded telling insights on the challenges that public servants and senior bureaucracy faced in this Prime Minister's initial reign of which, beyond Canberra's 'chattering classes', the wider Australian community was entirely unaware.

Across many years, our shared communication has been a source of happiness. We have the closeness of friends who speak of things, both great and small, in an intimacy which is deeply precious to those who live alone. Change comes, and I am off to Paris to spend rich weeks with my friend in her new post of international collaboration. As Virginia Woolf's 'Mrs Dalloway' thoughtfully affirms: 'Friendship or the lack of it is going to be what it will all turn on in the end'.

As an author, one's books, even after long currency, can open roads to friendship. When early in the 1990s I returned to live in Canberra, the distinguished Canberra potter Cecily Gibson called me on the telephone. She had read my illustrated book *'A Bright & Savage Land'* and there was both delight and laughter in her voice. With Cecily, laughter was never far away. She was a rare independent who, bred in the Depression years in an impoverished yet loving Catholic family in the country town of Yass, had emerged as one of life's eager participants. Initially she trained and worked as a nurse, caring at one time in Canberra as she was proud to tell – for John Curtin when Prime Minister. She had also served as a very young matron in a remote southern rural settlement of New South Wales until the moment when she was shown, and had held, a Japanese pot in her hands and discovered her life's passion.

Having learnt professionally at potter Henri Le Grand's Canberra studio, she set off for Japan in the late 1950s to study Japanese pots, to master the ancient skill of the kick-wheel, and to blend the rigorous, ancient techniques with her individual Western style. In Kyoto, from her glowing talent, she became the chosen pupil of one of Japan's 'national treasures', the great potter Tomimoto Kenkichi, and won high reputation for her work. Back in Australia, she built a house, a kiln and gallery in Canberra, and following a Churchill Fellowship to South America, added Columbian art to her store. She enjoyed renown for the distinctive pots which she moulded from the local clay.

I did not know her then. I met this small mettlesome artist, some years my senior, only after a crippling accident, when a runaway car had crushed her at her garage door of her Queensland home. No longer able to use the kick-wheel to make her pots, she had returned to Canberra. There, surrounded by her beautiful creations, she lived an engaged life warm in communication. Publishing an autobiography, *The Gift of Fire and Clay*, in 2000, Cecily set down her independent creed which, amid the prevailing ambience of focussed ambition and greed, honoured a simpler past. 'We Australians', she wrote of a generation reared in the 1930s, 'knew who we were. We could think for ourselves. We knew that everything had to be paid for and only the air was free. We navigated our own paths and, on the whole, had more happy and fulfilling lives than people seem to have today. Our own small rung on the ladder seemed all right. We kept our dreams simple and attainable'. Yet she was keenly alive to Australian accomplishments in her past half century – in art, music, science, broadcasting, literature and education. It made her a vigorous companion. Her life illustrated what could be achieved coming from a brood of eleven children, brought up in hard times by a strong and solitary mother whose initials, 'ME', Cecily adopted as the hallmark signature on her pots.

Cecily Gibson was a rare acquisition in the friendships of my later years. Several of her beautiful pots, flickering with memory, now share my house. Among them I find a large, chunky brown soup-cup which, as the winter winds howl outside, I hug and drink to her.

Connection and affection can spring up in unusual places. Early in this new century, when facing the major operation to remove my cancerous kidney, and needing care for my first week of convalescence, Dymphna Clark had lent me Wilma Robb, a truly remarkable woman, who for several years had been an integral part of the Manning Clark household. Into my house swept this capable, ragged woman, who swiftly prepared my dinner and when, fragile, I turned in my bed to sleep, leant across to kiss me and said, 'I love you'. I long remembered its comfort and warmth. Thereafter, Wilma and I, along our criss-crossing paths, became familiar friends. I had enjoyed the good fortune of coming from a home where my parents loved and encouraged me in all my ways. But Wilma came from an impoverished family, scraping a hapless life together in rural New South Wales, with a mother too ill from cancer to care for her and a violent, haphazard father whom she learnt to resist. With her siblings outsourced among the extended family at the age of five, she was placed in care at Dalmar Wesley Mission, a Sydney Welfare Home for unwanted or unmanageable children.

It marked the beginning of a fragmented childhood spent in temporary rural foster care, attending primary, but not secondary, school, and the emergence of a frustrated and wilful child. At thirteen she ran away from home and, pronounced 'uncontrollable' and 'exposed to moral danger', passed into a series of increasingly oppressive Welfare institutions – Ormond, near Thornleigh, where hard labour scrubbing floors with a toothbrush was the order of the day and, after escape and recapture, Sydney's

Parramatta Home for Girls. Here – an institution guarded by immense, high walls, and internal regimentation – was a place from which Wilma could never break out. It was 1961.

Rebel and protester, Wilma was noticeable from the start. There, in an establishment that had begun its life earlier as the Parramatta Female Factory for convict women, she experienced the full impact of the management style of a malevolent institution – the kickings and bashings from which she carried the evidence of smashed front teeth and a broken nose, the long periods in isolation, and other violence. Yet in this mindless world, where, she recalled, 'we were told all the time we never had minds to use', nothing could break her spirit. After five months she was removed at night to the new and even more repressive Institution for Girls at Hay in rural New South Wales. Now she would learn what real punishment was. 'I was scared at Parramatta', she relates in an Oral History interview at the National Library in 2009, 'but in Hay I was petrified. I remained petrified all my life'.

At Hay, the litany of a system of enforced silences; forbidden eye contact between inmates (a method of psychic control honed early for male convicts at Port Arthur Penitentiary); marching; standing to attention; clicking heels; toilets and cold showers kept open for observation by male staff; solitary confinement; and the application of strong drugs designed for the mentally ill (which Wilma fought to spit out), shaped the outlines of her days. 'It was like seven days a week never changed from one day to the other', she recalls. 'We never knew the time. We never knew what day it was. We didn't know what each girl was there for. We didn't know where they came from'. After five months she was returned to Parramatta for a brief period but, still fighting, was back again to Hay. As a survival recourse, confused and depressed, she 'shut down'. She carried the legacy of 'dehumanisation' all her days, a legacy shared by most of the other inmates. 'It was criminal', she reflects, 'I became frozen in time, forever'.

As our friendship grew, I knew Wilma outwardly as a successful carer and a loving single mother of three children. I only slowly came to recognise the depth of her personal trauma. Protected in my comfortable life I had no real idea of the depth of her experience; here was true vulnerability. 'If you damage a child', she summed up, 'you damage a person forever'. In the last years, however, I have watched a miracle unfolding. In this new century, Wilma Robb has become an articulate representative of the scattered groups of young girls whose experience in the '50s, '60s and into the early '70s was mirrored in brutal establishments across Australia.

Poorly educated and burdened by memories, during 2004 she made a handwritten submission to the Senate Inquiry into Children in Institutions (stirred by Senator Andrew Murray, himself a former British child exported to Zimbabwe) which detailed her time between 1961 and 1965 – from the age of thirteen to seventeen – spent at Parramatta and Hay. In it, she carefully recorded the names of her abusers, employed in their different capacities by the NSW Government Department of Community Services, including one doctor and one psychiatrist. 'I would like to ask now', she said there, 'if these monsters in "Experiment in Child Welfare" were handpicked and given books of rules or were told to do whatever they chose to do'. 'We need to be heard', she declared and offered her submission for public use. While both institutions at Hay and Parramatta were shut by 1974, the records of their infamy have been closed for seventy years for the ascribed purpose to 'protect the privacy of the inmates'!

I follow Wilma on her crusade as she broadcasts her experiences on television and radio, at TAFE Colleges and in museums, setting her sights with those of former colleagues that such events can never happen again. In this, they may be less than sanguine. An exhibition on 'The Forgotten People', staged successfully at the National Museum of Australia in 2013 with the women's active participation was originally refused a place in most of the State museums across Australia. Wilma's response, however, is far from passive. When in November 2009, Prime Minister Rudd delivered a formal apology in the Commonwealth Parliament to 'The Forgotten People' – a company of some 500,000 Australians who suffered ill-treatment, malpractice and abuse in orphanages, children's homes, religious establishments and State Welfare institutions across the land – and promised that they would be given special entry rights into Old People's Homes, a pleasing outcome for many, Wilma's protest was terse and strong. 'We've had enough of institutions', she cried, flashing a strong banner at Parliament House, 'it's compensation we need'.

A rebel still, Wilma has made a major journey while, for me, a dark piece of Australia's history now underwrites our strong connection. Enriched by her wisdom, I am most fortunate to have her as a friend.

In a long life, the presence of a friend of some six decades who links past and present, circling from a shared and eager young womanhood to old age, is testimony to the power of enduring friendship. In our salad days, Alison Cox and I shared a mews flat with two others in London, tucked in behind the Station of Gloucester Road where the sound of the tube trains rocked us to peaceful sleep. Our lives beckoned deliciously. She worked at the BBC, I then at Chatham House, and, having fallen in love with England and the handsome Michael Cousins, I was soon putting the question to her 'Should I marry him?' 'Yes', was my friend's firm reply. But feet on ground, she herself later married an Australian orthodontist with whom she would have children, travel, acquire wealth and property, and experience much contentment. Back in Australia following my brisk English marriages, our differing lives – Alison's as a key figure with Tresillian Association for mothers and babies, and mine of the scholarly kind – knitted into long companionship.

In recent years, our husbands no longer alive, we have been journeying together across what Prime Minister Deakin rightly called a 'country of magnificent distances'. Attaching ourselves to the *Spirit of the Outback* we have stitched together the map of Australia that has moved us from Perth to Broome, around the towering Kimberleys, through the cragged surfaces of the Northern Territory, to the bare inland and the Flinders Ranges, to Lake Eyre, and across the length and breadth of Queensland. Such journeys have often touched the themes of my historical writings. My 'historian's boots' have now made contact with the indented coastlines and coastal rivers of north-western Australia, which the captains of Dutch, British and French ships mapped – casting their own and their naturalists' names on the coast and countryside; the flat unremitting landscape where Burke and Wills came within a modest mile of the Gulf of Carpentaria; and places where the name of lost Ludwig Leichhardt nods at us unexpectedly.

On our final journey into Western Australia's vivid red Pilbara – where rock-scapes etched with ancient Aboriginal carvings are heaped together around the contours of the mines – we have been exposed to the stories of the indigenous people and to their sharp encounters with white settlers. Behind the rich

Pilbara mine looms the massive 'No name Mountain'. 'No name mountain', I exclaim, 'what about its indigenous nomenclature? Is this 'No Name' not a double insult?!' Yet, returned to Canberra I find to my dismay that one of Australia's most famous artists Fred Williams has painted the mountain under its crude 'No Name' styling, in a work given advertising prominence at his retrospective exhibition at the National Gallery of Australia.

But as we leave the rich Pilbara mine, in a neighbouring Tourist Park we read the tenacious words, framed on the wall, of an Aboriginal elder, which linger in my mind: 'We have a culture never change. You can do what you like on this land, but whatever you do, this land never change. They think they can do anything with it, but in the end maybe this land might turn on us'.

CHAPTER 15

OLD AGE

I first began to take an interest in old age, theoretically speaking, in the 1970s when Simone de Beauvoir published her *Old Age*, the first book by that single title. I remember that just before its publication in a Penguin edition in 1977, de Beauvoir was interviewed by the media and told the story of how, sitting on a beach, her gaze had fallen on some elderly figures and she experienced the sudden recognition that 'I will look like them soon in my old age'. The story stuck. I had read with lively interest her earlier books, the dynamic, internationally celebrated *The Second Sex* (1949), her first volume of autobiography, *Force of Circumstance*, followed by an ironically titled book (for the real picture was quite the reverse) *A Very Easy Death*, about her mother.

De Beauvoir's *Old Age* was in every sense a pioneering book. Writing as the 1970s opened, apart from specialised work there were, she asserted, no works anywhere referring to 'the old' who, in both France and the USA, were dismissed and consigned to decrepitude. Conditioned by society's attitudes they had no sense of life as 'a grant in perpetuity'. No respecter of customs, de Beauvoir decided to break what she saw as the conspiracy of silence. Yet, breaking it led her down two paths: one where the dispossessed aged were called on to bear societal disregard and 'show serenity'; the other the path adopted by a cluster of distinguished

French elders – writers, philosophers, scholars, painters – whose careers of talent had brought them reputation. Many whom she addressed, in fact, as their afflictions grew, dealt quite miserably with old age, but a number showed vim.

'Voltaire's opened-minded approach', she recorded crisply, 'earned him a fine old age, despite his cruel infirmities'. Sigmund Freud, ill and the subject of numerous operations, continued to look forward, ready in old age to evaluate the phenomenon of ageing itself and to draw his conclusion that 'the desire for everlasting rest is not primordial or elementary; it expresses the need for getting rid of the feeling of inadequacy that comes upon the old, especially in the smaller details of life'. Freud, indeed, exhibited a strikingly adaptive modernity. While psychoanalysis was banished in Germany in 1934, and his books were publicly burnt in Berlin, he left the country for England in 1936 after the *Anschluss* and discovered amid the need to have his jaw and palate removed and a mechanical jaw installed – how widely famous he was. He now confirmed that his earlier theories had been mistaken and accepted that the hysterical women patients who came to see him had not been raped by their fathers; rather, they dreamed they had been raped and 'that was more interesting'. Error led him on. There was, he believed, 'an eternity to make the most of'. He died not long afterwards in 1939.

Monet also enthusiastically embraced old age. Although with dimming sight he could no longer see colours with precision, he never stopped painting, 'his memory', as de Beauvoir observed, compensating for the failure of his eyes. In his great old age, his sight returned entirely and he produced some of his most astonishing masterpieces. When he painted his self-portrait very late in his career, there he was, 'upright and merry, loving life, his eyes, full of gaiety'.

Strangely for the author of *The Second Sex*, her book is entirely male-centred despite the existence in the late 1960s of a number of distinguished older women who had embraced neither failure, total domesticity, nor decline. Nevertheless Simone's perceiving eye observed that for all of us in older age, there is that sense that we remain unalterable to ourselves and cherish the belief in an essential being who lives on inside us. 'Nothing', as her life companion and lover, Sartre echoed buoyantly, 'will ever make me quit my own skin'.

De Beauvoir's book, with its culturally dispiriting evidence, now seems curiously dated. What then of Australia's historical experience? As the historian Graeme Davison so memorably reminds us, in its early years of settlement Australia was 'a society without grandparents'. His comment freshens the historical scene. But, with the advance of time, old age became a grim struggle for the poor and undereducated elderly in colonial society, where the concept of a 'useful life' held persistent sway. Federated Australia, however, showed leadership when, in 1908, the Commonwealth Government introduced the Old Age Pension as one of the earliest acts of the new Australian Commonwealth. This legislation officially placed ageing at sixty-five for men and sixty for women and, in the parlance of the period, provided for those who carried a 'legacy of hardship and fear'.

In 1901, however, only a modest four per cent of the population had reached sixty-five. By the 1950s it had doubled to eight per cent. Even so the picture remained bleak. State mental hospitals in Australia had become receptacles for unwanted old people, regardless of their state of mind and, as historian Stephen Garton records, women were three times more likely to find themselves incarcerated there than men. The interwar years were particularly unkind to older women, who were linked in the public mind to a loss of sexuality, femininity and childbearing. Not surprisingly, there was evidence of passivity and inertia among the aged.

I have been reading Katie Holmes' *Spaces in Her Day*, a study of the diaries of a number of women of the 1920s and '30s whose lives reflected the strong feminine commitment of women to a prescribed domestic dailyness where, in a community sense, women were marginalised. Yet Holmes found that – even as they recorded the 'insistent domestic detail' of each day – the women used the diary, and the space its writing afforded, as a realm of resistance to the prevailing conditions, and a place where they could define and shape their identities. As they aged – into the 1940s and '50s – their writings exposed their concern with age as a time of decay and loss of control over their bodies, and an awareness of life closing inwards. These were not predominantly negative accounts. But as the future shortened and the past grew longer, loneliness presented as the aspect of old age that most found difficulty in accommodating.

The study *Old People in a Modern Australian Community*, published in 1954 by the visiting British sociologist Bertram Hutchinson, was to transform attitudes to old age in this country. Seeing old age as a social problem, Hutchinson offered a psychological framework for 'successful ageing', where the individual's readiness to adapt were knitted into a positive whole. How rapid our sequential cultural change has been. Fifty years on, as senior citizens have gathered a prominence and a social category of their own, one hears the cry, '80, the new 60; 60, the new 40'! Even so, despite good health, a new cultural awareness and medications of every kind, the words of Alex Miller have true cognisance: 'It is not death', he affirms, 'but old age that is a foreign country'.

My own experience of old age has been very privileged. My parents passed their good genes on to me. And for many years I have been a great 'age-denier', slashing and adjusting years, pushing my luckless university confrères out of kilter, rephrasing my history. But no matter. If you are a writer of Australian books, the National Library of Australia, assigning authorship, offers your date of birth with a significant waiting dash at the front of each publication. Yet I hold the view that much depends on how you present, and how you think and act. 'I never thought I'd be old', Joe, my husband, said to me in unexpected wonder when he reached 80. Intellectually he never was. And for many years I have heeded a voice from the distant past. Sitting at the window of her anchorite cell in the days of the Black Plague, Dame Julian of Norwich greeted those who stopped there with the spirited words: 'All will be well and all manner of things will be well. Go forth gladly and gaily'. They, at least for the present, remain my touchstone.

Born in 1926, I belong to a generation where opportunities were opening but where most women still opted for the domestic life of marriage. Not opting, I now have a great regard for the grace and adaptive spirit of older women, the 'sixty-somethings' and older who have reared children, had part occupations, have been carers, and whose course has been different from mine. They are the flux of women who in their maturity have grown braver and freer as they aged, less interested in the opinions of those they have mentally left behind, no longer – as were those sisters of the

'20s and '30s – marginalised and under-recognised, but ready to take risks. They are the eclectic readers and absorbers, the participants who tread the corridors of our museums and art galleries, attend public lectures and Writers' Festivals; who support social, community and international concerns and are passionate about issues – women of a 'certain age' whom the writer Robert Dessaix calls 'the country's unsung intellectual heartland'. Australia is rich in them.

Yet as a long-time professional I accede to Simone de Beauvoir's personal precept, 'the greatest good fortune, even greater than health for the old person, is to have his world [note the pronoun] still inhabited by projects'. Writing history remains my project and my continuum, my bulwark against boredom and loneliness, a committed and engrossing world. That 'antlike meticulous labour', as Virginia Woolf called it, which carries one on until that chapter, that article, or that book or essay is finished and sent on its way and the next one in view.

David Malouf, passionate and eclectic creator of fiction, memoirs, essays, librettos, poetry – all much derived from history – acknowledges that writing is 'a kind of addiction'. 'If you are a writer, it's very, very hard to give up the business of writing', he declares, 'because physically in itself it becomes what you do and what you need to do to keep yourself healthy and thinking and alive'. I wave an assenting hand. It is an addiction and I admire those who can cheerfully set down their pen. Yet I rarely feel more secure or contented than when I have Roget's *Thesaurus* in my hand.

I was thirty, travelling on a plane from London to New York, when I first heard Voltaire's prescient phrase, 'So much to do, so little time to do it'. The voice who uttered it belonged to a surprisingly articulate (and, as it proved, determined) colonel in the British Army communications and intelligence at the War Office, Colonel Mozley who, flying above the world in an adjacent seat, had quoted it to me. I found it, and him, strangely attractive and, while my subsequent marriage to him lasted little more than thirteen months, Voltaire's message stuck.

But I think often, too, of Virginia Woolf's 'Mrs Dalloway', a cherished and protected wife preparing elaborately for her sixtieth birthday party, entertaining friends at her London home. Her mind travels back and forth across her years and the people who have delighted and influenced her. 'What a plunge is this business of life', she murmurs among the banked carnations. Yet for her, 'the compensation of growing old was simply this: that the passions remain as strong as ever, but one has gained – at last! – the power which adds the supreme flavour to existence, of turning it round, slowly, in the light'.

Have I come to do this in my old age? My love affair with M. illuminates the question. After ten years of close companionship, we came to part. It was my impulse that drove our parting, for as I admit in *Breakfast with Beaverbrook*, I have the ingredients in me of a 'bolter'. Yet 'relationships mean different things to different people', M. had said, and it was he who had initiated ours, surprising me with the specifying term. Yet, after its time of rapture, we both came to view it differently. 'You have always expected and wanted more from this relationship than I', he would say several years on when I, keen in the search for intimacy, was delving into its interstices.

Yet a relationship has a momentum, it must change and move towards a point of known commitment. Ours was a happy but loosely structured one in which we inhabited separate houses and pursued our independent careers. But George Eliot, my ever-ready prompt and guide, has one of her feminine characters observe: 'I like not only to be loved, but also to be told that I am loved. I am not sure that you are of the same mind'. And so I found it. Or is it as the distinguished jurist Michael Kirby, putting his finger on Australia's social mores, discerned: 'Anglo-Celts (and especially the males of the species) find the little word "love" terribly hard to say'.

Are women illogical, forever trying to reconcile emotion and life? Australian film director Ray Lawler addressed it in his evocative film *Lantana*, now a multi-award winning classic that resonated with audiences in Australia and abroad. Central to it were the relationships between three sets of women and two men and the deep longing of women to feel needed and loved. Their men, conversely, were bemused and irritated by this 'need' and one, so paralysed by the difficulties it created, was unwittingly responsible for his wife's accidental death.

Watching it again on a home video, I took notes. 'I want more than that', says the central female character of her static relationship with her policeman husband. 'Why do women always want to know what you're thinking', a man asks, clear in his belief that he is being manipulated. 'Most Australian women I know', says another female, 'find men decidedly other, another species'. It struck a chord. Yet perspectives flicker and change. Musing after M.'s and my parting and 'turning my reflections slowly in the light', I remembered the words of that discerning female writer A. S. Byatt in *The Game*. 'One must never ask for more than is offered – not out of virtue but because if one does one loses what one has'.

The reflection, flickering across landscapes and language, came into focus again as I watch a video of another brilliant film *Out of Africa*. There they are – the venturesome, independent Karen Blixen and the fascinating-but-roving Dennis Finch Hatton, one of those adventurous reserved Englishmen who inhabited Africa in the 1920s and earlier, and whom love entwines. As their love deepens, he is much away on safari choosing his times of coming and going and she, forever waiting, asks that he spend more time with her. 'I hoped you would never ask for that', he says. I sat up. There was to be no compromise. Even as she asked, she had become, I could see, less appealing. I knew it all. Dennis was killed in a flying accident a few days later. Had he not been, it would, no doubt, have changed nothing.

M. and I had an important shared history and much happiness. My photo albums, put aside now, bulge with reminders of halcyon times. But, growing old, it was a time for closer and more leisurely companionship. It did not come. 'Work, children and Ann', that old refrain, remained intact and with M.'s children and rising grandchildren far distant (how strong the blood-tie is), I would spend long periods alone. Like Karen Blixen I longed for a more committed share of time. Then, at last, I could not see myself cursed by expectancy, waiting for a desultory phone call tailored to M.'s need. 'You have the whole jug', said one of my younger friends wisely, 'but it's a small jug'. It was a question of how far one wished to be on the edge. Although it involved loss and deep sadness, it was not for me. M. nested then for several years near his family in another State. But he died alone.

'It takes two years to get over a broken relationship', said one acquaintance cheerfully. And so it did. One is losing one's once best friend. Bolting at 80 seemed unnaturally pioneering and I drowned myself in work. 'We will both be pleased in three months', said M. meeting me along the track, a mixed and tangled message. But there was something about 'the persistent self' that had stirred me. I have no doubt that, in one sense, it has been my innate choice of independence that has been both my strength and my compass error. Despite elegy, there is something about being in one's own skin.

Aloneness, however, is a journey; one must go the extra mile. I ask my older women friends, widows and those who are now partner-less, of their experience. 'One step forward, one step back', says one, and another, 'You just have to deal with it every day'. And from many, 'it's very lonely'. 'The future shortens, and the past grows longer'. Others, well-heeled city dwellers, tie their lives into series of concerts and plays, each day an experience and a solace. Still others in Canberra, Australia's volunteering heartland, reach outward, binding volunteer work into their days. One talented retired scientific woman on her own tells me that she makes a point of spending part of a day at a grace-and-favour desk at a university and the other part working and drawing at home. But she ensures if at all possible that she goes out in the evening when her whole day has been spent at home. Yet deep loneliness is clearly a formidable presence in our ageing society. For many 'sixty- or seventy-somethings' and their older sisters, the ABC Radio National is their companionable inheritance, offering stimulus and a sense of others, its importance crucial and its range empowering. Long may it remain! 'We collect ourselves', said Patrick White of old age, sober and crisply wise, 'as far as is ever possible'.

Chapter 16

OUT OF THE WEST

Sometimes in a lifetime a truly exceptional woman steps upon one's stage. International travel, academic leave in stimulating places, swelling armies of expatriates overseas, all break our geographical boundaries. Such a one for me was Fay Gale. She was a cultural geographer and a woman of remarkable dimensions.

Born at Balaklava, South Australia, Fay was the daughter of former Methodist missionaries, and with her father's move to Adelaide as a Methodist minister and her mother's spanning involvement, she made early contact with young Aboriginal women brought from remote outposts who came to share her bedroom at the family home. She took up the study of geography at the University of Adelaide (the first honours student to do so), she focussed her PhD degree on part-Aborigine women living in urban areas scattered across South Australia. And (pressed by their mothers and their growing concerns) she addressed the problems of young Aboriginal men, and their lack of protection and equity in the justice system which she published under such titles as *No Relation, Poor Fella: The City Aborigines' Dilemma*. Fay Gale was the first academic publicly to use the term 'the Stolen Generation'. All her succinct writings addressed problems and solutions that were ahead of her time and, communicated by radio and early TV interviews, drew both criticism and acclaim. They also had policy carriage, and with Don Dunstan's encouragement, passed into such legislation as the Land Rights Act of South Australia and the founding of the Institute of Aboriginal Studies. A rare and outstanding scholar and teacher, Fay became the first Professor of Geography appointed at the University in 1978. It was said of her that 'she made geography speak'.

I met her in London in 1985 when we were both staying at International House in Mecklenburgh Square and enjoying the luxury of having desks at the Australian Studies Centre then attached to London University. At that time, Fay was on another mission visiting England as a consultant on one of her other areas of expertise (taken up initially to study the impact of tourists on Aboriginal sites and later at Uluru) on tourist management, to advise on Stonehenge, and control the movement of tourists around the great brooding circle. The aim was both to establish a sense of heritage and personal connection through the purchase of commemorative items from an Information Centre and to prevent the assault on this historic relic by marauding tourist hands. While experts on heritage buildings in Britain were legion, Fay brought her special knowledge of how to deal with historical sites in open countryside.

When we met, she had recently undergone a traumatic divorce from her Methodist minister husband, reliant on her financially, but given to taking off with a series of young women. She became fearful of his continuing demands and had sought separation. But, in the light of her academic position and income, she had become a 'reverse precedent' in a new South Australian divorce statute that required a husband as breadwinner to divide his estate equally with his wife. Now the caring wife would incur the same duty, but freed at last emotionally and intellectually, and with her two children under her care, Fay had left the marital home with only a small suitcase and her car. As an outcome, when we met, her hair had turned quite white and she covered it with a wig. Together we found much pleasure and companionship on the London scene and when, a few months later she visited me in Sydney, I was enthralled to see rich brown hair curling upwards from her crown.

Not surprisingly, she became a high flyer in academia, her life full of 'firsts'. Appointed Pro-Vice-Chancellor at the University of Adelaide in 1988, she was the first woman to join the senior management team there and had been elected a decade earlier to the Academy of the Social Sciences of Australia. She found it dauntingly male. Already aware at the University that while undergraduate students in geography were 50/50 female and male, most women were caught up at tutor level. Her election to the Academy was her first conscious encounter with an all-male environment and she was 'not impressed'. It made her a dedicated and strategic feminist. In 1990 she was appointed Vice-Chancellor of the University of Western Australia, the second woman in Australia to hold such a post, the first being Di Yerbury at Macquarie University.

We would meet through the nineties as Fay passed professionally in and out of Canberra, enjoying rewarding talks, and after she retired in 1997 from the West, I did a long Oral History interview with her for the National Library of Australia, which involved reading her published work across a cascade of research interests on cultural geography, demography, indigenous subjects, the environment, heritage, conservation, women, and social-theory themes and found it totally absorbing. It was the most candid interview I ever did. With her background in Aboriginal affairs and indigenous rights and, known as an outspoken critic and reformer deeply opposed to the ongoing bureaucratisation and amalgamations which, under John Dawkins as Minister for Education, was significantly altering the scholarly role of Australian universities, Fay discovered, to her surprise, that her name had cropped up, uninvited, on the University of Western Australia's Selection list. Attending the interview, it was not an appointment in that 'frontier' State that she expected to get. But she was chosen unanimously. 'I didn't want the job', she said. But buoyed up by the information that the Appointment Committee really wanted me, 'they told me it was unanimous', she would soon find that the conflicts she encountered in the West were 'absolutely huge'.

It made riveting reading. Two of the three deputy vice-chancellors, with strong internal connections, had sought the job and made it clear that one of them should have been appointed. By contrast, Fay went into the situation knowing no one, and with no one she could trust. The opposition, silent or loud, she recalled, 'was very strong'. A lone woman, without friends in the West and placed in the Vice-Chancellor's huge six-bedroom, five-bathroom house, she was 'very, very lonely'. 'It is very isolating', she reminds us, 'at the top'. But she was destined to become a pre-eminent figure in Perth. Across seven years in the 1990s would move that traditional sandstone university of an outpost State into the highest academic echelons in Australia, the elite 'top eight' – winning major research grants, strong showings in national university quality-assurance review programs, and collaborative research efforts with industry – and leave a major stamp on a spread of innovative projects that included many to advance the career opportunities for women.

In this she proved a warrior and a rebel. 'I had to force it', she said. Her reforms turned on the diverse discrimination experienced by women students, providing basic recognition and support for women against discriminatory practices and policies. They brought in childcare services, the provision of a plan for the safety of women on campus at night and, importantly, an examination of the entire field of PhD supervision for women – an area that had become the subject of serious concern in the under representation of women candidates and their treatment by male supervisors. The bright young male, said Gale, 'is always seen as a much better catch than a woman who is slightly older on account of taking time to rear children'. It was difficult for women who have families; it was difficult for women who were single because it is a lonely life. She knew from experience of both. As Vice-Chancellor she was persistent in forcing these developments, setting out to get a critical mass of talented senior women. When, seven years later, she left, there were sixteen women professors, a good number of senior women, and many administrative posts run by women. They became known affectionately by women students as 'Fay's Way'.

In 1996, Fay was appointed President of the Australian Vice-Chancellor's Committee, the first woman to hold the post in seventy-five years, and in 1997, the year she retired, she established the 'Fay Gale Fellowship' with an initial grant of $1 million which recognised the disadvantages caregivers experience in caring for children, aged parents, and spouses, and which, in the vast number of cases, although not all, were awarded to women. They were exceptional achievements. Will it last, Fay reflected, when men inherit her position as Vice-Chancellor, Deputy and Pro-Vice-Chancellor? But she had noted, over and over again, among Aborigine women, among women in Africa ('where women do everything and men do nothing'), that when things are really bad, 'the women club together to do really marvellous things'. And she could see that 'beginning to happen in universities'. Her role was transforming. Resolute, open to change, she continued in retirement to reiterate her themes on the Aborigines and her understanding of their careful occupation of the land before the arrival of white settlers. She remained optimistic. 'I have never thought that just following', she said, 'was exciting'.

Yet, counterwise, as Vice-Chancellor she also encountered the most searing hostility and controversy, and a sustained vilification from the press for her equity plans which raised the ire and opposition of a predominantly male culture still clinging to its strong frontier mentality. Attending formal occasions she would emerge to find her car covered with dog excrement; her name attacked in black capitals in the press the next day; her achievements sullied but hard won.

With her retirement Fay experienced another 'first' when elected in 1997 as President of the Academy of the Social Science in Australia, the first female to hold the post. And there with her strong interdisciplinary concepts, she initiated important joint projects on immigration; on management plans for Kakadu, Uluru, and the Burrup Peninsula in the Kimberley; and other problems, with the Australian Academy of Science in which her constructive, interrelated approaches marked the purposefulness of her reign and evidenced a holistic contribution to society and society's issues. Essentially she was a path finder.

Several months after her retirement from the West, I attended the farewell party which the leading women staff of the University of Sydney gave Fay Gale: a time for praise and celebration. And there she spoke with frankness of the challenges she had experienced as Australia's second woman Vice-Chancellor in that 'othersider' State. For despite her pride in becoming a Vice-Chancellor, it had also been, she recounted, 'the nastiest, most bitter and loneliest job in her life'. At her frank revelations, the University's hosting Chancellor, Emeritus Professor Dame Leone Kramer, turned her back on the speaker and declined to notice her eminent guest. Yet it was entirely consistent with Fay's dedication to share instructive knowledge that she pulled no punches in the Oral History interview and left her buoyant tape and transcript open for researchers.

Fay Gale died in 2008, her loss to the community great. She was a woman of undaunted courage and ability. As my own mind runs currently and I write on the explicit need in Australia to adopt interdisciplinary approaches to address the 'wicked' problems that confront us humanly and scientifically in a complex scientific age, I think often of my friend and how valuable she would be to have among us. For she believed that it is in the learned academies, rather than in the competitively structured universities, that real collaboration and exchange can be effected. Were she here, she would make an ideal Chief Social Scientist, a practice now adapted in Britain. She calls for a discerning biographer.

CHAPTER 17

WAVING TO BEAVERBROOK

It can be argued that in everyone's life there is an individual who has loomed larger than any other; one perhaps who has taught, cared for, mentored, protected, influenced even overborne perhaps or inspired. Who was that person for me? My answer to the question comes swiftly. Across my life there has been such a one: the dynamic and controversial Lord Beaverbrook after whom my earlier memoir is named. The things he taught me flow through the chapters of this book – to be independent; not to take establishments and the established as seriously as they take themselves; not to be snowed by authoritative figures or 'mini-men'; and to examine and question the sources of power. From his own vivid life, he added, 'put irons in the fire', 'take risks'. And so I have made my way.

Beyond certain media and political circles, the name of Lord Beaverbrook – powerful long-time proprietor of *The Daily Express, The Sunday Express* and *The Evening Standard,* and Churchill's resourceful Minister of Aircraft Production in the Battle of Britain – has faded largely into history. In my earlier memoir, *Breakfast with Beaverbrook,* I wrote about those vivid days between 1954 and 1958 when I worked with him in London and around the world, researching and assisting in the writing of *Men and Power* which propelled him to international acclaim. So compelling, indeed, was the success of this history of British politicians and their struggle with the generals in the last two critical years of World War I, that Beaverbrook went on to write several other works of political history and to cherish the hope – overriding all other aspects of his fame – that he would be remembered for his books. He died in 1964 at the age of eighty-five.

And so, in 2010, having myself entered the decade of Lord Beaverbrook's final years, I decided to travel to England to visit the British Parliamentary Archives at the House of Lords which house the Beaverbrook Papers and take a retrospective look at his record of extraordinary achievement. My motive here was threefold. First I wished to go back to that time, more than fifty years ago, when, my spirits soaring, I had cut my political historian's teeth on some of Britain's major historical papers which, through wealth, ingenuity, and foresight, Beaverbrook had gathered to his exclusive use. I also wanted to discern how this contact and experience had shaped me, and to refresh my recollection of the passion and interest of those heady days – when World War I became 'our war', and that old revolutionary song 'bliss it was in that time to be alive', rang in my ears. But, above all, as a senior and experienced historian, I wanted to look at the work we had done together – work which had made so important an impact on Lord Beaverbrook's life – and gain an understanding of the place this major figure in British affairs held in a field where he is less widely known: as a historian.

When I joined him as his personal research assistant in 1954, he had already published two historical volumes entitled *Politicians and the War 1914–1916*. These told of the political events and upheavals of those two first years of World War I that had culminated in Prime Minister Asquith's ejection from the seat of power in December 1916, and his replacement by David Lloyd George who brought Great Britain to victory. As Max Aitken, a successful Canadian entrepreneur, Beaverbrook (he was elevated to the House of Lords in 1919) had come to Britain as a twice-made millionaire in 1910 and rapidly entered the House of Commons. There he became the intimate friend of fellow Canadian Bonar Law, leader of the conservative British Unionist Party, and an insider who would play a critical role in the stratagems that, with Aitken's collusion, unseated Asquith. With an eye to political history, Beaverbrook had kept a detailed record of these events and, capturing recollections of the period from key participants, he had drawn his two early books together as a vivid episodic story in 1928 and 1932.

Essentially, he was writing a particular kind of history. It was not, as he put it, a history in the strict sense; rather, it dealt with the highlights that shone on big events and on the vital decisions of the personalities who took part in them. Framed as it was between memoir and history, academic historians paid it scant attention. But by 1954 Lord Beaverbrook, had set a new and ambitious course. He planned to prepare a series of works that would cover the political events of World War I from 1917 to 1918, move on to 'The Age of Baldwin', and conclude with a study of 'Churchill and the Second World War'. For this, through personal contacts and private purchase, he had built up a unique documentary empire. It contained the papers of the brief-term British Prime Minister Bonar Law, who had died in 1921, and bequeathed his papers to his friend; the papers of David Lloyd George purchased from the Countess Lloyd George (George's long time secretary); the papers of Lord Curzon; and his own considerable archive, covering his participation in British political and media life since his arrival in England.

Such documentary riches, to the annoyance of Britain's ivory-tower historians, placed Lord Beaverbrook in the unrivalled possession of the richest stock of British twentieth-century political papers in the country. The academics dubbed them the 'Nibelung hoard' (after the hoard of gold guarded by a dragon in *The Ring Cycle*) and contended that, a newspaperman at heart, Beaverbrook would set about a form of historical brainwashing. This was the scene into which I entered in some ignorance in 1954. I was twenty-seven; Lord Beaverbrook had just turned seventy-five. On meeting the small, lively figure with a puckish face, he declared gaily, 'I mean to lead my life as if I am seventeen instead of seventy-five'. He did.

Now, more than half a century later, here I was ensconced in the Records Room at the House of Lords, London, and engaged in an absorbing journey. The elaborately catalogued Beaverbrook Papers, some six-hundred-and-sixty-six boxes, stretched before me, holding his complex and varied political, business, and international dealings, his immense private correspondence, and the details of a lifetime across seventy action-packed years. But for me it was the 'Historical Boxes', themselves a line up of forty-seven large containers, that for several weeks became my private domain. Opening the first box I was met at once by my old typescripts and those first crisply succinct messages that Lord Beaverbrook, travelling abroad, would send me, typed up in characteristic blue typescript from his SoundScriber at the office of the *Daily Express*.

Brooking no delay, Lord Beaverbrook – having selected me from a large group of potential appointees – had installed me in a small office at the *Daily Express* and set me the task of overviewing all the memoirs that had appeared in print since his publication of *Politicians and the War 1914–1916* some twenty-five years before. 'I have now seen all the reviews of your two volumes', I reported in my earliest communication in August 1954, while he lingered in the south of France, 'and know the main targets of attack which seem to be remarkably few'. Working diligently, I had gone on to find that Beaverbrook's first-hand accounts of those wartime political manoeuvres for power and place had been accepted by most of the other players as their source for accurate recollection; and in so doing, I had formed a scholarly base for the writing of his proposed third volume on 1917–1918, which we would tentatively call *'Politicians and the War', Volume 3*. 'The material is admirably arranged', he replied (to my relief) 'and I look forward to receiving more material which I shall discuss with you on my return'. Our long conversation had begun.

Because of his close involvement in the action, our method of working together was destined to take a form very different from the more traditional manner of historical research (in which a research assistant scurries about exploring the raw material and presents their notes to their employer to adapt). In this case it was Lord Beaverbrook's extraordinary memory of those far-off events that provided the structure of our approach. I have described our methods in my earlier memoir, and find that they have passed into at least one course on Historical Methodology in Australia – that run by Professor Stuart Macintyre at the University of Melbourne – where they evoke, I am told, both considerable interest and 'a sense of being positively Edwardian'. I repeat them here:

'By normal methods we worked in reverse. In conversations, walking in Green Park, or standing at his high upright desk, he would recreate for me the outline and atmosphere of a political incident and illuminate with stories and anecdotes the personalities involved. A born raconteur, with a flair for a pungent phrase, his staccato style was contagiously easy to acquire. My mind taut with concentration, I would hurry off to grasp my typewriter before the spoken version lost its freshness and bite. Against the lively outline drawn from Beaverbrook, I would check his recollected account against his diaries of engagement, consult the secondary sources, and draw together the documentary material, the letters, notes and memorandum which the talented archivist, Sheila Lambert, dug from the manuscript collections. Her work was crucial to the scheme. A trained historian, recently married to the distinguished Cambridge Tudor historian, Geoffrey Elton, Sheila was a young north-country woman, bouncing with energy and a keen professional grasp of the resources within her care. She had catalogued the Papers of Bonar Law and was working on those of Lloyd George. Plump, her greenish eyes would sparkle with zest and sharp intelligence as the hunt began. Against this more complex framework, I would concoct and type up the chapter's first draft. This draft, taking at times new directions and elaborations of Beaverbrook's original account, in turn, stimulated him and the result resembled an exciting snowball thrust back and forth with gathering pace'.

Now the evidence of our incessant work flowed from the Historical boxes. Lord Beaverbrook's historical enterprise had quickly captivated his mind. Working through the collected material, I found it bursting with the record of notes, expanded and rewritten drafts, new material, references, incessant communications from the itinerant author, responses from participants invited to comment, and a plethora of Beaverbrook's amended galley proofs and final book proofs – his favourite (if highly expensive) form of revision – as new inputs arrived. Once again, Lord Beaverbrook was writing a particular kind of participant history. It was not just a chronology of British political events in the last two crucial years of war. His interest lay in men's behaviour in the discharge of their ministerial roles and, in a period of great national peril, in their struggles for power. In time, as the autumn leaves fell about the campuses of Yale College and Harvard University, I was contentedly installed among the manuscripts held in their splendid libraries searching out evidence which, as only Beaverbrook suspected, would lie in some private diplomatic correspondence. It invariably did, and there were the notes which I had made from the Colonel House Papers and others which formed key elements of the book.

In making my reconnaissance, I was amazed at the span of revision, the updating, the rectifying and extending of drafts, the scrupulous attention to detail, and the search for and receipt of corroboration of facts and actions. The documentation was vast; Beaverbrook's hand was everywhere. He absorbed new information supplied by me, and wrapped it carefully into the text. When other commentary was received, Sheila Elton would repair to the archives to verify it. Examined against the documents of the period, his accuracy was outstanding. Moreover, his knowledge of the personalities and incidents gave him a mastery over the documentary material that no other historian, working systematically through the records, could hope to achieve. Again, the traditional methodology where the writer begins with the historical documents and inches forward with the narrative was acted out in reverse. Reviewing it, I recognised that I was now at a singular vantage point. It was exhilarating, as the one-time participant and now an experienced historian, to pin down in detail the unique mode that placed Lord Beaverbrook so distinctively in command of this piece of British political history. Other biographical historians could make their independent analysis and judgment of the material with hindsight in the years ahead, but Beaverbrook's involvement as a historian was unique.

There was another aspect of Beaverbrook as a participant historian and archival manager on which my latter-day sortie shed light. During the early 1950s, with his growing cache of political papers, he had commissioned two biographical ventures from the papers written by journalists: *David Lloyd George*, by the *Daily Express* journalist Frank Owen, and a second by Leonard Mosley, *Lord Curzon: The End of an Epoch*. But a third, and the most important, biography, of his close friend and political hero Bonar Law, he consigned to the rising Oxford historian Robert (later Lord) Blake. My searchlight on the papers now illuminated the growth of the relationship between these two extremely different men: one a powerful and keenly interested patron, the other an 'up-tight', teetotal young don from the heartland of academe, Robert Blake.

Beaverbrook had given Blake untrammelled access to the Bonar Law Papers and the assistance of his talented archivist. In turn, Blake submitted his many chapters to his patron. At first Beaverbrook maintained a scholarly rectitude. But dashing off SoundScriber messages from the south of France, he was soon playing a seductively interventionist role. Despite fortitude, Blake soon fell under Beaverbrook's spell. His sponsor's strikingly retentive and accurate memory, borne out in Blake's recourse to the papers, struck him compellingly and their discussion was detailed and rich. 'I am interested in what you say about Carson. Carson remains the most puzzling character', Blake wrote in 1953, 'and I would like to discuss it in detail when we meet'. In time the don was enjoying Beaverbrook's excellent and lavish hospitality.

To Blake, Lord Beaverbrook offered the same vivid advice for a historian which he had later bestowed on me: 'Never wait until you accumulate all the evidence before you take up your pen: write before you become bored and the subject becomes dead. Tell the tale in the proper chronological order with plenty of dates. Begin at the period which most interests you: you will have to write it all again anyway'. It was advice, Blake later reported, that he passed on to all his doctoral students. His substantial *The Unknown Prime Minister: The Life and Times of Andrew Bonar Law, 1858–1923* appeared to the acclaim of scholars in 1955.

After a day locked in the two men's lively exchanges, I would set off home on the Underground to Baron's Court, where a new Queensland friend offered me a welcoming hearth. The April flowers bloomed brilliant yellow and mauve in the leafy old cemetery which I crossed from the station, while frisking squirrels played among the tombstones. As I walked I reflected on those historical days and the men who had played their engaged parts in them.

'Our book', *Men and Power*, was published in 1956. As 'Mrs Ann Cousins', Beaverbrook gave me warm acknowledgment. But by the time of the book's appearance, I was 'out', swiftly despatched from Lord Beaverbrook's side over my planned marriage to Colonel Mozley, so I was not aware of the widespread reviews the work had received or its impact in positioning Lord Beaverbrook as an important figure on the historical stage. *The Manchester Guardian* saw the work as 'quiveringly alive' while Lord Templewood (Samuel Hoare), reviewing it in *The Spectator*, characterised it as 'an absorbing thriller whose plot is the rescue of a country from terrible danger'. The scholarly Blake, addressing it at length in *The Sunday Express*, judged that 'On any view Lord Beaverbrook's performance is an extraordinary one. He has written something that is, in the true sense of the word, unique. It is unlike any previous historical work ever written by anyone – even by Lord Beaverbrook himself'. Lord Beaverbrook, he observed, 'was now much more than a writer of particular episodes and crises in which he played a part, he brings to them the accuracy and scholarship of a true historian who has really studied and understood the great collections of historical papers both in his own possession and elsewhere'.

It was, however, the verdict of the renowned Oxford historian and public broadcaster, A. J. P. Taylor that gave Lord Beaverbrook the greatest satisfaction. Writing in *The Observer* that Christmas Eve, Taylor named *Men and Power* 'the outstanding book of the year'. Once something of a public critic of Beaverbrook, Taylor had now experienced a profound conversion. For him, Lord Beaverbrook had become the 'supreme narrator of political conflict...to which the new evidence from his stock of papers heightened the drama'. 'This', Taylor pronounced, 'is high politics at their most ruthless, presented by the greatest ringmaster of the age'. It was the beginning of an intimate and enduring friendship between these two men, revealed in Taylor's letters of deep affection which I found in the Beaverbrook Papers.

Their conversations greatly enriched each other; Taylor was made an Honorary DLitt of the University of New Brunswick where Lord Beaverbrook ruled as Chancellor, and ultimately became Beaverbrook's literary executor and biographer. 'Lord Beaverbrook's friendship', he summed up in his major biography

Beaverbrook in 1972, 'enriched me. The joys of his company are beyond description...I was not important in his life except perhaps by appreciating his historical works at their true worth... Now that I have learnt to know him better from his records I love him even more'.

These glowing collective opinions of *Men and Power*, viewed after many decades, gave me enormous pleasure. I had been aware – when Lord Beaverbrook wooed me back after my short failed marriage to Colonel Mozley to join him in the summer of 1958 at his villa 'La Capponcina' in the South of France when Sir Winston Churchill was his cherished guest – that the reception of his book had lifted him to a different plane. In former days he had been somewhat tentative in writing history, dependent on collaboration and, despite his special knowledge and insights, eager for encouragement and support. Now, with his new confidence, we were happily embarked on his proposed next volume 'The Age of Baldwin' and working on those dynamic days when the Duke of Windsor, determined to win out against Prime Minister Baldwin and make Wallis Simpson his morganatic queen, had found support and assistance in Churchill and Beaverbrook, those two 'King's men'. 'The Age of Baldwin', however, did not mature, and Taylor would edit and publish Beaverbrook's spirited account of the Abdication as *The Abdication of King Edward VIII* posthumously in 1966.

Other books would flow from Beaverbrook's pen; his last, *The Decline and Fall of Lloyd George: And Great Was the Fall Thereof*, was published in 1962. Taylor thought it not of the same quality as *Men and Power* and recommended that Beaverbrook extract some of the overstocked letters which (declining the advice) the author popped into an Appendix. Yet D. G. Brogan summed it up crisply in review: 'More and more historians are coming to see that the venerable nobleman, even if he places himself at the centre of the stage rather more than as an observer from outside, is providing a most valuable source for the secret history of the First World War'. But by then I was far away in Australia at the ANU and on the receiving end of Lord Beaverbrook's correspondence and published works. And the planned final book 'Churchill and the Second World War' (for which the audience was huge) never took form. Walking among the playful squirrels, I was tempted to wonder would it have done so, if I had accepted Beaverbrook's invitation to stay with him.

It had proved a richly informing time among the archives. History had beckoned beguilingly in many guises. Walking each day beside the Houses of Parliament I would pass the powerful figure of Cromwell astride his sturdy horse, and gaze with a familiar nod at the towering sculpture of Winston Churchill looming across the square. I had talked, too, with lively shared interest with Jonathan Aitken, Lord Beaverbrook's great 'nephew' (through his Canadian cousin). A handsome man of 66, Jonathan was a former Minister and Parliamentary Secretary to Margaret Thatcher's government who, in 1999, had quite famously left the Parliament to spend several months in prison for perjury. There he found God. In 2011, he would open Lord Beaverbrook's curiously shabby country home, 'Cherkley Court' in Surrey, to the public.

During his lifetime, Lord Beaverbrook had clung tenaciously to his archival 'horde'. He was, he said, 'an old man in a hurry' and would maintain his hold. After his death, his manuscript collection made up of his own vast archive, the Lloyd George Papers and the Bonar Law Papers found their way to the new Beaverbrook Library in St Bride Lane near Fleet Street where, under A. J. P. Taylor's honorary directorship, they were opened to enthusiastic scholars. But late in the 1960s threatened by sale to an American university by Lord Beaverbrook's son, Sir Max Aitken, at the financially troubled *Daily Express*, they were spirited away by Taylor and placed in the House of Lords Records Office. And there, as the Clerk of Archives proudly informed me as I left, the Lloyd George and the Beaverbrook Papers have become the Parliamentary Archives' 'best sellers'.

Through his fierce commitment, Lord Beaverbrook had clearly cut a singular path through the political history of World War I and, from intent and purpose while others slept, had positioned himself 'in command of history'. As archival proprietor, patron and participant historian, he was unique. In twentieth-century terms, he had emerged as 'a historical one-off'. His books now evoke the wide admiration of scholars. Early in the opening of his papers a trio of Canadian historians questioned his accuracy on the fall of Asquith in his early *Politicians and the War 1914–1916*. But as his later biographer, Anne Chisholm, concluded in her *Beaverbrook: a Life*, written with her husband Michael Davie in 1992: 'For students, Beaverbrook's accounts remain essential reading. They will continue to do so because they are an excellent, and often the only source for certain transactions'. 'Besides', she added, he 'never wrote a boring paragraph'.

My visit had proved both enriching and confirming. In particular it gave me special pleasure when the British Journal, *History Today*, with its wide international circulation, gave prominent place in its 60th anniversary issue of January 2011 to my article on Beaverbrook titling it 'The History Man' and carrying Lord Beaverbrook's historical reputation far on its way.

EPILOGUE

Horace's ancient injunction *carpe diem* – 'seize the day' – has for centuries been a potent and civilising guide. But there is a less often spoken corollary, *obire diem* – 'to meet one's day'. I believe there is no contemporary writer who has offered a more direct communication on this than Australia's public intellectual Donald Horne. Having given us books – both personal and penetrating – on education, politics, government, leadership (or lack of it) and the sociology of 'the lucky country', he bestows upon us *Dying: A Memoir*, published with his wife Myfanwy. It is a celebration of life, offered with a view, so rarely afforded, from the disappearing bridge. Through their long and happy marriage, Donald and Myfanwy Horne have set store in mixing a close familial companionship of themselves and their son and daughter through journeying, picnics, food prepared with enjoyable care and celebrations. Now, equipped with a tape recorder, Donald set himself the difficult task of noting the progressive stages of his ebbing days. Along with the growing challenges, they track the dailyness of the passage. 'I know', he adds endearingly, 'that some of what Myfanwy and I are having is much the same experiences as people have anywhere, with new machines to use, new people, all subjects for good talk. In a strange kind of way, we continue to build our experience'. On the final edge of old age, as a sense of isolation and fleeing control grip him, Donald Horne has given us a special gift.

Advancing old age offers the impulse for calm scrutiny and the turning of the balance sheet. Goethe's reflection, however, was singularly bleak. 'We look back on our life', he wrote, 'as a thing of broken pieces, because our mistakes and failures are always the first to strike us, and outweigh in our imagination what we have accomplished and attained'. I think not! For while I am aware of the failures and the abortive and wasted efforts that litter my past, I also see this time of scrutiny as one for gratitude and celebration. Reflecting on history, enormous change has taken place in Australia in its study and compass since, at the tail end of 1958, I returned from Britain to participate in the founding of the *Australian Dictionary of Biography*. The eighteenth volume of this monumental work has just rolled off the publisher's press, encapsulating in its density and breadth the singular advances in our knowledge that have lifted us from our early preoccupation with convicts, governors, explorers, and bushrangers. It now embraces a highly diversified multicultural, industrialised society, enriched by the presence of the indigenous people; by diversely based women participants; scientists and technologists; a maze of professions and scholarly disciplines; creative figures across the arts; and a medley of players in governance, business, education, administration, sport and politics, with a sprinkle of quirky or colourful individuals, who have enhanced and broadened our national life. It gives us, in sum, the story of the Australian people.

An overview of this vast collective scholarly enterprise – *The ADB's Story* – which, across over half a century has drawn upon the voluntary contributions of Working Parties, authors, researchers, librarians and willing contributors from every region and State, has now been published by ANU Press and records this unique venture's place both as a renowned 'jewel in the Australian National University's crown' and as a loving account of this long and continuing national endeavour. I am proud to have played a part in its crucial 'establishment days'.

From my own ringside seat, I have also watched the history of Australian science become part of the mainstream of Australian history, spreading through university courses and post-graduate studies, through national and international conferences, and into an outpouring of books and papers undreamed of when I launched the study in 1962. Now the 'Bibliography of the History of Australian Science', presented biannually in the disciple's major journal *The Historical Records of Australian Science*, can muster a hundred or so new entries twice a year. It's a veritable 'hold bag' of Australasian history that enfolds the natural sciences; the 'enabling' sciences of physics, mathematics and engineering; technology and innovation; anthropology; and biography, autobiography and the sociology of science – a range that offers us an extended conversation with our past. For me, this outpouring of research and knowledge underscores my persistent belief that history illuminates contemporary concerns.

Across my professional career I have kept a keen eye on the progress of women in science in Australia. In *'A Bright & Savage Land'* I first drew attention to a pioneering cluster of nineteenth-century women – Georgiana Molloy, Louisa Atkinson, the intrepid German collector Amalie Dietrich, the Scott sisters, Harriet and Helena, and Ellis Rowan – who, while contributing to knowledge and popular interest in the country's flora and fauna, had remained for long among the 'silences' of 'Australian science'. Science was a patriarchy. Yet unschooled in botanical theory or in the emerging debate on evolution versus fixity of species which male investigators in Australia were beginning to explore, these women and other unnoticed sisters responded individually to the beauty of Australian nature and depicted the variety they saw. Their observations and delicate illustrations added an important, but largely disregarded, dimension to the story. In recent decades, however – to my delight – the 'silences' have been shattered, and the once 'invisible participants' have been taken up for biographical attention. Collective studies have also emerged of women botanical and natural-history artists, garnered from the rich resources of the National and State libraries.

There is evidence of some frustrating losses. From the late 1980s I came together with a talented group of young women researchers and burgeoning historians of science in Sydney and Melbourne to frame a collective work that would trace the differing roles played by representative women in the emerging disciplines of science. My valued colleague and research assistant Elizabeth Newland and I widened the search by inviting generalist-science-journal readers to send names of relevant women from the late nineteenth and the twentieth century, with biographical notes. We reaped an abundant haul. Well armed, we submitted a detailed proposal to the Australian Research Council (ARC) for funding to assist the publication of a collective work. But the project, strongly endorsed by a high-profile woman sociologist, was rejected by a male referee who wanted a different kind of book. In the prevailing male-dominated culture of the period, this important venture fell to the ground. There has been further research and the record of women's advances in science remains a fertile field. But it is unfinished business, and as the materials assembled for the science women's collective are deposited in the

Basser Library of the Australian Academy of Science as 'Women in Australian Science', I flag them here.

During 1995, a group of leading science women (and myself, as a historian of science) were called together under the aegis of the Chief Scientist in Canberra to prepare a Discussion Document titled 'Women in Science, Technology and Engineering'. We met for lively exchange on several occasions but our Report in May, with its unequivocal pronouncement of the existence of 'Gender Harassment in Science', perhaps prompted its early disappearance to a dusty bureaucratic shelf. By 2012, however, there was evidence of change. A coterie of scientific women had risen to hold professorships in the Australian universities while some seven per cent of women currently make up the fellowship of the once wholly male bastion of the Australian Academy of Science.

In this twenty-first century, however, we must pause to re-assess. In a country that has yielded its first woman Prime Minister; first woman Governor-General; first woman Commonwealth Chief Scientist from 2009 to 2011; Chief Scientists in New South Wales; the first woman President of the Australian Academy of Science; and women directors of Australia's three major scientific organisations, CSIRO, ANSTO (Australian Nuclear Science and Technology Organisation), and the prestigious Walter and Eliza Hall Institute of Medical Research – can we assume that the 'glass ceiling' for scientific women has, in fact, been broken? Is this a trickle or a defining trend?

What emerges is a paradox. Recent research in which I have participated has confirmed that in both Australia and industrialised countries overseas a historically shaped culture has emerged where high women achievers arise but the majority of women in science remain cooped through multiple career barriers such as childbearing, fewer publications, a lack of mentoring and professional exchange, in the lower employment ranks while their male peers move traditionally upwards to senior scientific posts. The culture of gender differentiation is entrenched by women's lack of confidence and self-esteem and by a prevailing unawareness by men that such gender disparities exist. At root there is need for major attitudinal change. But let us go forward with hope.

Having myself chosen early to leave academia and become an independent scholar, it has been a singular relief to leave hierarchy behind. Position is irrelevant; recognition of real account. And so I have spent the past twenty years of my professional career at a desk in the 'Petherick Room', the site of the Special Collections at the National Library of Australia. It was the foresight of the early National Librarian, Harold White, and his belief that a community of scholars was a vital part of Library affairs, that led to the creation of this special place – where scholars find quiet and welcoming space and the ready assistance of librarians. For me, seven of my books have emerged from 'the Petherick'.

Tucked into the National Library, I also began my long association with its creative Oral History Program, conducting interviews with Australia's leading twentieth-century scientists, an experience that opened my eyes to the sociology and key trends of twentieth-century science, and introduced me to some of Australia's greatest scientific minds. It was then I learnt, at first hand, that many of our key scientific men had come from simple backgrounds, often rural; that almost invariably they had strongly supportive mothers; and that a cluster had made fertile use of the long-established Mechanics Institutes in country towns to stimulate and shape their direction. Like all pioneering research, it had been both enlarging and instructive, and my *Portraits in Science*, an edited collection of twelve of these interviews with some of Australia's most significant scientists (Professors Fenner, Oliphant, Nossal, Ringwood, Messel, Bishop and Slatyer), published by the National Library in 2004, is now available on the internet.

And so I tick my balance sheet. For most of my life I have been somewhat tentative about academic recognition, early abandoning my plans for a higher degree at London University and placing the lure of interesting employment above the acquisition of a PhD. But encouraged by a friend early in this century, I presented my collected book publications to the Australian National University for consideration for a higher degree, and was greatly honoured when in 2003 they bestowed the degree of Doctor of Letters on me. Four years later my own alma mater, the University of Sydney, presented me with an honorary DLitt that marked sixty years since my graduation in history in 1947. Receiving it at an Arts Graduation ceremony in the Great Hall where the portraits of successive Vice-Chancellors gaze benignly from its walls, my mind flew to the time six decades before when, as a final year honours' student in history, I did my last examinations in that illustrious hall. Now, a robed elder (surely quite the oldest on the podium), did my old Professor of History and one-time Vice-Chancellor, Stephen Roberts, I wondered, smile briefly down on me?

Addressing those eager Arts students that day, I took as my theme – a recurring one – the division that had grown up in Western society since World War II between the two cultures of science and the humanities which C. P. Snow had brilliantly focussed in his book of that title. Snow saw this 'polar divide' between the two mindsets as particularly 'dangerous'. Viewing it as a historian of science who has sought to unite science and its historical context across my career, I see it as vastly more dangerous today. And so my message to this assembly of bright young humanities and social-science graduates (some already involved in interdisciplinary fields in their postgraduate research), was to urge them to bring their talents and diverse skills and insights to the problems and challenges that confront us in an increasingly complex scientific age. Their contributions as engaged participants will matter greatly in the years ahead.

Along with science, history will surely lie at the heart of that contribution. As the eminent Canadian historian Ronald Wright reminds us in his wryly titled *A History of Progress*, amid the wreckage of past civilisations, 'we need to keep our eyes on history and to change our ways'. Similarly, Australian Nobel Laureate Peter Doherty in his *The Beginner's Guide to Winning the Nobel Prize* has also underlined: 'It is not only scientists who have the future in their bones'. For me the answer will always lie in an interdisciplinary approach in which the values and knowledge and the foresight of the humanities and the social sciences – of behavioural scientists, psychologists, humanists, geographers, demographers, historians, economists and those who represent the arts are melded together with science in a holistic approach to what are now defined as the 'wicked problems'.

There are deeply challenging elements in these problems. As the only species in the planet's millions of years of living history who has managed to obtain dominance over other species and impose patterns upon a universe, *homo sapiens* has much to learn and re-address. We may need to find a new descriptor for *homo sapiens* who, in a small slice of time of little more than two thousand years, has wreaked profound havoc and exhaustion on Planet Earth. Recently, Emeritus Professor Christian de Duve of Belgium's Catholic University of Louvain, another Nobel Laureate for his work on cellular structure, has concluded in his book *Genetics of Original Sin:* 'Natural selection has resulted in traits such as group selfishness being encoded in our genes'. These judged as useful to our ancestors under the conditions in which they lived, he suggests 'have become noxious to us today. You need wisdom to sacrifice something that is immediately useful or advantageous for the sake of something that will be important in the future. Natural selection doesn't do that, it looks only at what is happening today'. De Duve sees some possible routes to salvation in ethically and scientifically applied population and birth control. But he also considers giving more power to women who, less aggressive than men and playing a larger role in the early education of the young, 'can help them understand their "genetic heirloom"'.

Can we hope to affect such long-term change? Late in life, Charles Darwin, I find, made the sanguine forecast that 'man in the distant future will be a far more perfect creature than he is now'. The case is open. Certainly, my own historical researches among the Australian fauna, the koala and the platypus, firmly underwrite the belief, pressed urgently in Australia by Tim Flannery and others, that 'the earth is not only for humans'.

In my early Canberra days, two young interior decorators advised me wisely that if you lead a lively life, come home to quiet colours. In old age, personal joys draw one closely in. What pleasure I find in my Canberra home in my sitting room. Serenity and tranquillity linger here. 'Regret little, and resist despondency', writes British author Diana Athill of old age, at ninety, in her book *Somewhere Towards the End.* The words of Australian poet

Timoshenko Aslanides, from his poem, 'Things Worth Having', resonate in my ears:

> *Cheese, fresh bread and old Sauvignon Blanc.*
> *Subjects that disagree. Verbs that will govern any case.*
> *Present so extended by conversation*
> *As to be future perfect. Life, settled in gender*
> *And in number. Thin wine glasses. Friends.*

INDEX

Adams, Phillip 43, 105
Aslanides, Timoshenko 198
Aitken, Jonathan 187
Athill, Diana 197
Baker, Don 42, 64–65, 146
Banks, Joseph (Sir) 15–16, 20
Bassett, Jan 52
Baudin, Nicolas 1, 15, 21
Bauer, Ferdinand 20, 117
Bennett, George 110–113
Blainville, Henri de 117
Blainey, Goffrey 11
Blake, Robert (Lord) 183–185
Bowring, Ian 108
Broinowski, Alison 41–42
Brown, Robert 4, 117
Brunton, Paul 146
Byatt, A.S. 166
Caldwell, William 112–113
Carlyle, Diane 146
Chambers, Wade 21–22
Chatfield, Elly 94–95
Charlesworth, Max 40, 42
Chisholm, Anne 188
Childe, Gordon 92
Churchill, Winston x, 186–187
Clark, Dymphna 63, 65, 69–77
Clark, Manning 9, 56, 60–64, 70, 74–76, 80, 83, 89, 153

Clark, Sebastian 74, 76
Clarke, Patricia 37, 42
Clarke, John 146–147
Clarke, Maria 139, 146
Clarke, W.B. 5, 28, 65, 73, 135, 140, 142, 144–147
Clear Across Australia 26, 36, 66
Cox, Alison 156
Cook, Patrick 119
Coombs, Nugget 39, 73
Cousins, Michael 124, 157
Crawford, Max 9, 22
Cunningham, Allen 15
Cuvier, Georges 110–111
Daintree, Richard 141
Dame Julian of Norwich 163
Dana, James Dwight 136
Davison, Graeme 10, 161
Dark, Eleanor 88, 90, 94, 108
Darwin, Charles 19, 37, 95, 112, 135, 144, 197
De Beauvoir, Simone xi, 108, 159, 164
De Duve, Christian 196
Dening, Greg 10, 22
Dessaix, Robert 164
Doherty, Peter 196
Encel, Sol 42
Eccles, John (Sir) 12, 97

Eliot, George 165
Elton, Sheila 182
Flannery, Tim 197
Fleay, David 120
Flinders, Matthew 4, 117
Freud, Sigmund 160
Gale, Fay 169, 173–175
Garton, Stephen 162
Gibson, Cecily 151–152
Gilbert, John 16
Glendenning, Victoria 96
Gould, Charles 140
Gould, John 4, 16, 140
Governor Gipps 139
Greenwood, Gordon 9, 58
Hancock, Keith (Sir) 11, 56–57, 59, 98
Headon, David 37–38, 42
Heidler, Irmgard 44
Heilbrun, Carolyn ix
Holmes, Katie 162
Holmes, Richard 85, 120,145
Home, Edward (Sir) 110
Hooker, William and Joseph 16, 19, 112
Hooton, Joy 38–39, 42
Horne, Donald 189–190
Hoyle, John 101–102
Hoyle, Mary 102
Hurley, David 121, 131
Hurley, Doss and John 1–2, 122
Hurley, Mimi 26, 31,34, 55, 121–13i; as Mary Hurley on the Sydney Stock Exchange 125
Hutchinson, Bertram 162
Huxley, Thomas 19, 106, 140
Independent Scholars Association of Australia (ISAA) 40–45

Iremonger, John 41–42
James, Clive 81, 148
Jevons, Stanley 144
Jones, Barry 42, 103, 105
Jukes, J. Beete 138, 140
King, David 94
King, Phillip Parker 15, 112, 135
Kramer, Leonie (Dame) 175
Krefft, Gerard 120
Lamberton, Don 104
Lamarck, Jean-Baptiste 110–111
Law, Bonar 178, 181, 183–184, 187
Lawler, Ray 166
Leichhardt, Ludwig 17, 138, 157
Lesueur, Alexandre 21
Lewin, John 117
Lord Beaverbrook x, 2–3, 10, 53, 57, 77, 105, 176–188
M. 46–55, 75, 98, 146, 149–150, 165–167
Macintyre, Stuart 59, 180
McLeay, Alexander and W.S 5, 135
McKernan, Michael 42
McQueen, Humphrey 38, 42
Mander Jones, Phyllis 20
Malouf, David 164
Manning Clark House 75–76
Mansergh, Nicholas 10, 57
Martin, Stephen 144
Meckel, Johann 110–111
Miller, Alex 163
Modjeska, Drusilla 129
Monet 160
Moorehead, Alan 77–87
Morrison, Alastair 99
Moses, John 38, 42
Moyal, J.E. (Joe) x, 23–35, 51, 53, 77, 97–98, 126, 128–129, 163

Moyal, J.E. Lecture and Medal 35
Moyal, Schemuel and Nora 26, 29, 31, 34
Mozley, Everest 124, 184
Mueller, Ferdinand von 18–19, 144–145
Murray, Les 65–67
Newland, Elizabeth 192
Nicholls, Brian x
Nolan, Sidney 83
Olley, Margaret xi
Owen, Richard 17, 110–113, 142
Parker, Nancy 97
Parkinson, Sydney 20
Pearce, Margaret 150
Peron, Francois 149–150
Perry, George 117
Pockley, Peter 106
Pocock, Tom 80
Poiner, Gretchen 42–44
Ralston, Edith 122–123, 125
Rea, Angus 146
Reid, Alan 104–105
Robb, Wilma 54, 153–156
Roberts, Stephen 10, 195
Ryan, Judith 26, 126–132
Sayers, Andrew 8
Sawer, Geoffrey 98
Scrivener, Charles 1–2

Sedgwick, Adam 133–137
Shaw, George 109
Snow, C.P. 11–12, 195
St-Hilaire, Geoffroy 110–111
Stevens, Margaret 38
Taylor, A.J.P. 185–188
'The Clever Country' Exhibition 3–8
Twain, Mark 116
Ulman, Vivienne 93
Varuna, The Writers House 88, 90–94
Ward, John 9
Webb, Jenny 148–150
Webster, David 34–35
White, Harold 194
White, Patrick 26, 80, 168
Whitlam, Gough 104
William Clarke College 147
Williams, Robyn 7, 21, 105–107
Wilkinson, Charles 141
Wilson, J.T. 5, 113
Woodroofe, Gwen 97
Woolf, Virginia 90–91, 127, 151, 164–165
Woolf, Leonard 90, 96
Wright, Judith 43, 73, 115, 132
Wright, Ronald 196
Yerbury, Di 171

www.ingramcontent.com/pod-product-compliance
Lightning Source LLC
Chambersburg PA
CBHW030343240426
43661CB00052B/1730